Dissertations

in

American Economic History

Dissertations

in

American Economic History

Advisory Editor
Stuart Bruchey

Research Associate
Eleanor Bruchey

*See last pages of this volume
for a complete list of titles.*

ALEXANDER HAMILTON'S FINANCIAL POLICIES

Mildred Otenasek

ARNO PRESS

A New York Times Company

New York / 1977

Editorial Supervision: LUCILLE MAIORCA

————◦◦◦∞◦◦◦————

First publication in book form, Arno Press, 1977

DISSERTATIONS IN AMERICAN ECONOMIC HISTORY
ISBN for complete set: 0-405-09900-2
See last pages of this volume for titles.

Manufactured in the United States of America

————◦◦◦∞◦◦◦————

Library of Congress Cataloging in Publication Data

Otenasek, Mildred.
    Alexander Hamilton's financial policies.

    (Dissertations in American economic history)
    Originally presented as the author's thesis,
Johns Hopkins University, 1939.
    Vita.
    Bibliography: p.
    1. Finance--United States--History.
2. Hamilton, Alexander, 1757-1804. I. Title.
II. Series.
HG181.O74 1977   336.73   76-39837
ISBN 0-405-09917-7

ALEXANDER HAMILTON'S FINANCIAL POLICIES

By

MILDRED OTENASEK

A Dissertation

Submitted to the Board of University Studies

of The Johns Hopkins University

in Conformity with the Requirements for the

Degree of Doctor of Philosophy

CONTENTS

ALEXANDER HAMILTON'S FINANCIAL POLICIES

It would be a vain attempt to write a biography of
the illustrious Hamilton. Lodge, Morse, Oliver, John C. Hamilton,
Ford and others have written adequately of the man's life. Likewise, many books have appeared depicting Hamilton, the statesman.
However, little has been written of Hamilton the financier. In
the writer's opinion, finance has been Hamilton's greatest contribution. He has left his imprint on all our economic, political,
and social institutions. But his greatest achievements have been
in the field of American finance and public credit. With no
precedent for procedure, Hamilton forced through his plans and
policies and organized the country's finances. Within five years
he established a national bank, a unit for the coinage of metals,
provided a uniform national currency, and devised a scheme of tax
yielding adequate revenues to sustain a huge national debt.

All this is incredible when we consider how few were
the active years of Hamilton's career, how unprecedented were
the tasks allotted him, and what obstacles he encountered. The
financial developments of the past one hundred and fifty years
owe their origin to Hamilton. His influence on the financial
development of the United States cannot be overestimated. In true
perspective, we can recall Gallatin's eulogy: "Results, legislative and administrative, were tremendous, and can never be
repeated. A government is organized once and for all and until

that of the United States fairly goes to pieces no man can do
more than alter the work accomplished by Hamilton". This successful achievement calls for an analysis, which the author plans
to make. It is intended to discuss Hamilton in the light of our
financial history. Chapter I will portray the period of financial
collapse -- Hamilton's heritage. Chapter II will be concerned
with Hamilton's financial ideas and plans -- a brief description
and a detailed account of their origin and development. Chapter
III will be a vindication of the attacks made against Hamilton.
Chapter IV will deal with Hamilton's contributions to the subject
of Political Economy.

The author has obtained much information from the two
editions of Hamilton's works by Lodge and is indebted to Senator
Lodge for his biographical notes. But primarily a debt is due to
Hamilton, for this thesis is essentially based on Hamilton's five
memorable reports -- the First and Second Reports on Public Credit,
the Report on the National Bank, the Report on Mint and Coinage,
and the Report on Manufactures. The Hamilton Manuscripts have
been of utmost importance in indicating the intensive work done
in the writing of the reports.

To have written merely an abstract of Hamilton's
financial views and the ensuing legislation, interspersed with
comments, would have been an easy but unsatisfactory task. A

financial treatise, in order to possess value, must trace the causes and consequences of legislation. Thus the author will not attempt to summarize the reports but only to give an abridged account of all of Hamilton's financial recommendations. The interested reader must have recourse to Hamilton's works for detailed information of his reasoning and proposals.

With respect to a few facts, the reader's indulgence must be sought. Sources of information, especially of our pre-Hamilton financial development, are in some parts contradictory, owing to the confusion which existed in the accounts of the old government. The most important facts, however, have been obtained with a considerable degree of accuracy.

The author is deeply grateful to Dr. Broadus Mitchell for the liberal use of his time and energy. This is a feeble acknowledgment for such valuable assistance. A greater satisfaction will be derived from knowing that if the work possesses any value, its readers are indebted to him for putting the author within reach of much of the material found in these pages. I should also like to acknowledge the kind assistance and encouraging spirit of my other professors. Their influence has been inestimable. Finally, my sincerest gratitude must go to my husband whose inspiration is reflected in every word.

CHAPTER I

Financial Collapse: The American Crisis

The present degree of organization and efficiency of
our financial structure makes it difficult for us to understand
the primitive financial system which existed before Hamilton
became Secretary of the Treasury. Alexander Hamilton received
his appointment on September 11, 1789. The period previous to
this date can be called "The Dark Ages of American Finance".
An enormous state and national debt, a heterogeneous mass of
currency, unsuccessful attempts at banking, coinage and mintage,
were Hamilton's heritage. There was little precedent and successful experiment for him to follow either in the colonial or
revolutionary period. To appreciate adequately Hamilton's
unenviable position, it will be necessary to review briefly the
state of credit, currency, banking, mint, coinage and the tariff
in the colonial and revolutionary eras.

During the colonial period, the finances of the country
were largely under the control of the British. This was fortunate
since it served as a check upon the ingenuity of the colonists.
Yet, repeatedly, we find one state and then another indulging in
"mad financing". This was particularly true with regard to the

currency issues. The first paper money was printed in 1690 by
the colony of Massachusetts.[1] Passed as an emergency measure,
in order to pay the soldiers returning from an unsuccessful ex-
pedition against Canada, it involved only 40,000 pounds. But
it was a fatal step and its apparent success led to grave
disorders. Although the issue was based on land and was to be
redeemed within twelve months, at no time did the currency pass
at par. Soldiers got rid of it at one-third discount.[2] Yet, this
new financial device spread through the colonies like an epidemic.
In Rhode Island the paper money was issued "to advance trade and
promote manufactures". This was in the nature of a loan bearing
5% interest and based on real estate mortgages, owned by those to
whom the money was advanced. 7000 pounds were printed in 1710;
40,000 in 1715; 40,000 in 1721; and another 40,000 in 1728, "on
account of the decay of trade and commerce".[3] South Carolina
printed bills in 1712 to meet war expenses. They steadily depreciated, falling a third the first year and a half the second.
New Hampshire, Connecticut, New York, New Jersey and Pennsylvania --
all issued paper money. Some of the provincial governors and
the legislatures were at variance with the "paper money issuers",
but were powerless to control their activities. Consequently,
these bills of credit, as they were called, in the course of time

[1] Horace White, Money and Banking Illustrated by American History, p. 120
Ginn and Co., 1896
[2] William G. Sumner, History of American Currency, p. 15
[3] Jacob Upton, Money in Politics, p. 15

brought on concomitant evils. They all eventually underwent the
same experience: emission, disappearance of specie, counterfeiting,
wearing of bills, collecting and replacing worn and counterfeited
issues with new ones, extending the time for old ones to run,
depreciation, repudiation of an early issue of paper money in
part, and emission of another disguised under the name of "new
tenor". Douglas, an authority on Massachusetts currency, says that
at one time Massachusetts had "old tenor, middle tenor, new tenor
first, new tenor second";[4] it is said that Rhode Island had an
indefinite number of tenors. Counterfeiting, wear and tear,
became inevitable and trying evils. The former was punishable
by death in most colonies but it is doubtful that the penalty was
ever enforced.[5] Counterfeiters set a new vogue by halving and
quartering bills and uniting a half part of a five pound note with
a half part of a ten pound one. There was no limit to their frauds
and tricks. The Acts of Parliament passed in 1750 and 1763,
forbidding the further issue of paper money, succeeded in minimizing
although not in abolishing this evil.[6] There was need for some
paper money, inasmuch as what little specie there was, had to be
sent to England for needed imports. But the colonists, sensing
the immediate success of paper money printing, issued without
limit or judgment. Thus, due to a lack of comprehension of the

[4] Charles H. Douglas, Financial History of Massachusetts ("Columbia
University Studies in History, Economics and Public Law, I, No. 4), p. 48
[5] White, p. 28
[6] Sumner, p.38

nature and limit of issue, paper money failed.

In the field of banking, the colonists made no such
disastrous experiments as they did with their currency. Their
few attempts to establish a bank to supply a medium of exchange
were always checked or suppressed by the colonial or home government before the ultimate economic effects had manifested themselves.
It will be profitable, however, to discuss these early attempts.
The earliest ideas of banking in the United States were drawn from
England. The company or partnership was the commonest conception
of a private bank in England. The general idea was that the bank
should issue notes with land as security and thus obviate the
necessity of redemption. No capital was necessary to start a
bank, only confidence. On this theory attempts were made to found
private banks in Massachusetts, in 1671 and in 1681.[7] Nothing is
known of their history. Five years later, plans were made for
another bank in the same state. The bank was to issue notes and
make loans on the "security of land and imperishable merchandise".
In 1733 the New London Bank of Connecticut was formed. A group of
landholders mortgaged their estates for the notes of the bank.
The Land Bank of Massachusetts, in 1741, was founded on the same
principle. Although unauthorized, it began operations, only to be
checked by Parliament's declaring that the old Joint Stock Company
Act passed in 1720 was to be effective in the colonies.[8] Thus the

---

[7] William G. Sumner, History of Banking in the United States, p. 3
[8] Ibid., p. 24

institutions were suppressed before they had become the instruments
of a new era of financial excesses. Strictly speaking, the only
banking that existed in this period was a type of lending. No
banks existed, banks in the sense of our modern conventional
institutions for receiving deposits, making discounts, negotiating
drafts, etc. In the words of Francis a Walker, "those banks
which existed, were a batch of paper money".[9] The issuers never
had a place of business, a specie reserve, or a corporate existence.

Equally barren was the colonial experience in coinage and
minting. It is said that the first attempt to establish a mint
was made in Virginia.[10] There is no proof, however, that a mint was
erected. Massachusetts had established a mint in 1652.[11] Here the
famous "pine tree shillings" were coined, so called, from the figure
of a pine tree stamped on them. Shillings, sixpences and three-
pences were struck for many years. The pine tree shilling,
however, contained only 72 grains of pure silver, the true English
shilling being 93 grains. This made ten pence to a shilling,
instead of twelve as in the English coin. Besides, the mintmaster
kept fifteen pence out of every twenty shillings coined, thus
reducing the coins an additional 3%. Consequently, they were dis-
counted at 25% immediately. A similar experiment in Maryland met
with the same results. In 1662, the Catholic Assembly of Maryland

[9] Francis A. Walker, Money, p. 317
[10] David Watson, History of American Coinage, p. 1
[11] White, p. 14

obtained permission from the proprietaries to set up a mint.[12] At
the very outset, the coins were 25% below valuation.

    With the tariff the colonies had had great experience,
chiefly as the victims of unjust oppression. The Navigation Acts
had had demoralizing results. They led to fraud, evasion, and an
open disregard of laws. Soon internal trade was substituted for
foreign trade as a means of evading tariffs. On the one hand,
while decrying the tariff activities of the mother country, the
colonists themselves began taxing each other. Nearly every
assembly had levied duties on tobacco, slaves, and liquors imported
from other states. Maryland prohibited beer, flour, and bread from
Pennsylvania.[13] Rhode Island taxed sugar imported from the
colonies. New York placed a duty on barrels. Georgia and South
Carolina put restrictions on lumber and bricks from the New
England colonies.[14]

    From these few instances, it becomes obvious how little
progress was made in finance during the colonial period. There
was little financial activity due to the simple organization of
society at that period and, also, because of the curbing influences
of the British crown. The little that transpired, however, was
uncontrolled experimentation which was decidedly primitive and
was by no means the forerunner of more acceptable financial
policies. The colonists made no positive contribution to

---

12 Upton, p. 10
13 Victor S. Clark, History of Manufactures in the United States, p. 59
14 Ibid, p. 60

American finance and gave Hamilton no basis on which to work.

Revolutionary finance was strikingly similar to colonial
finance. Both resorted to paper money to meet expenses. The two
differ only in degree. The chaos which faced Hamilton in 1789
was not the result of a few years of reckless financing. It was
the inevitable climax of a series of experiments carried out
during the century, begun by the colonial government and followed
with little variation by the revolutionary government.

In discussing currency, we might say that bad as the
colonial state of currency was, that of the revolutionary period
was far worse. And this would be true from the purely objective
point of view of modern finance. But when we look at the matter
from a purely utilitarian standpoint and consider the urgency
of the situation we see that the revolutionary currency, bad as
it was, nevertheless, served its purpose. Since there was no
other alternative at the time, we should not censure the action.
The need for money was urgent and had to be met. Even Benjamin
Franklin wrote a pamphlet favoring this method. An excerpt from
his autobiography shows his attitude toward the paper money when
it was first issued. "My friends there, who thought I had been
of some service, thought fit to reward me by employing me in
printing the money -- a very profitable job and good help to me".[15]

[15] Upton, p. 18

In 1779, he observed:

> This effect of paper currency is not understood
> on this side of the water and, indeed, the whole
> is a mystery even to the politicians, how we
> have been able to continue a war four years
> without money and how we could pay with paper
> that had no previously fixed fund appropriated
> specifically to redeem it. This currency as
> we manage it is a wonderful machine -- it per-
> forms its office when we issue it in pay and
> clothes troops and provides victuals and am-
> munitions and when we are obliged to issue a
> quantity excessive, it pays itself off by
> depreciation.[16]

Nevertheless, in discussing the origin and development of Hamilton's

fiscal policies it will be necessary to state facts, in order to

see the conditions previous to 1789.

On June 22, 1775, a resolution was adopted that a sum

not exceeding 2,000,000 of Spanish milled dollars be emitted by

Congress in bills of credit for the defense of America.[17] The

bill passed the following month. The 2,000,000 dollars were not

yet issued when another million was demanded and authorized,

together with more than 3,000,000 before the end of the year and

9,000,000 more before independence was declared. This was the

debut of the continental currency. By 1778, the emissions amounted

to 63,500,000 and 242,000,000 in 1779. In the final check-up in

1780, it was found that they reached a total of 357,000,000.[18] To

aggravate the condition, Congress authorized commissaries and other

[16] N. Sparks, Life of Franklin, VIII, 328
[17] Bartow Hepburn, History of American Currency, Macmillan, 1915.
[18] White, p. 135

officials to issue certificates of indebtedness for supplies
taken for the army and for other debts. Consequently, we
had a variety of currency: bills of credit, loan office certificates, indents, certificates issued by quartermasters, purchasing agents and commissaries. Provision had been made for
their redemption. The issues were to be met by taxes and loans.[19]
Unfortunately, Congress had power to levy taxes but not to collect
them. What little money was obtained from taxes and from foreign
loans by no means satisfied the expenditures of Congress. Consequently, the currency depreciated and, when thoroughly discredited,
was redeemed at a certain percent of par. Immediately a new batch
was issued with a solemn pledge for redemption at a given date,
only to undergo the familiar course of depreciation. On March 18,
1780, Congress passed a resolution providing for redemption of the
continental currency at 1/40th of its face value -- an act of
practical repudiation.[20] Later the low value of this currency
became more obvious when under Hamilton's Funding Act of 1790 only
6,000,000 of the 357,000,000 were funded at the ridiculously low
rate of one cent for a dollar. The remainder had probably been
lost or destroyed.[21] Of the bills issued by Congress, Breck says:
"Annihilation was so complete that the barber shops were papered
in jest with the bills. Sailors on their return from a cruise,

[19] A. Gallatin, A Sketch of the Finances of the United States, p. 123
[20] C.J. Bullock, Essay on the Monetary History of the United States,
[21] John W. Kearny, Sketch of American Finance (1789 - 1835) N.Y. 1887

being paid off in bundles of this worthless paper money, had suits
of clothes made of it and in characteristic light-headedness,
turned their loss into frolic by parading through the streets in
this decayed finery which in its better days had passed for
thousands of dollars".[22]

The writings of Peletiah Webster on this subject have
become classic. Of the paper money experiments, he wrote: "We
have suffered more from this than from every other cause of
calamity; it has killed more men, pervaded and corrupted the
choice interests of our country more than and done more injustices
than even the arms and artifices of our enemies".[23]

Although many favored further issue of paper money, no
one had any respect for it. Even Washington wrote to Custis
(October 10, 1778) advising the latter not to accept money for a
piece of land that he was about to sell, but to take other land
in exchange for it because the money might lose its value.[24]
He subsequently wrote "that a wagon-load of money will scarcely
purchase a wagon-load of provisions". The Mennonites absolutely
refused to accept currency. When they brought their produce to
the market, they would carry it from house to house and would sell
it at a very low price for hard cash but would rather carry it
home again than sell it for congressional currency. The Quakers

---

[22] Samuel Breck, Historical Sketch of Continental Paper Money, p. 15
[23] Peletiah Webster, "Political Essays", quoted in William G. Sumner,
History of American Currency, p. 45
[24] N. Sparks, Life of Washington, I, 132

likewise refused to accept the paper money and in many instances
they suffered fines and imprisonment, their stores were robbed
and their properties confiscated.[25]

  Occasionally Congress would address the people on the
financial condition of the government and would try to counteract
the mounting public debt with emphasis on the virtues of the country,
its extensive fertile territory, its good climate and great productivity. But all to no avail. The money depreciated still
further. As Jay wrote Washington, April 26, 1779, "The state of our
currency is really serious. When or by what means the progress of
its depreciation will be prevented is uncertain. The subject is
delicate, but the conduct of some men really indicates at least
great indifference about it".[26]

  Depreciation was enormous and all remedies seemed
hopeless. In 1781, a soldier's pay had dropped from $7.00 a
month to 33¢ although it was twice raised by Congress in the
year. To quote Sumner, "A man might lose his whole wages while
earning them".[27] With paper money becoming unmanageable, Congress
resorted to specific supplies to feed the army. Requisitions were
made upon the states for pork, beef, flour, corn, forage, etc.
Contrary to expectation, this was even less satisfactory, since it
called for a vast system of transportation, warehousing and

25 John Fiske, Critical Period of American History, p. 164
26 John Jay, Life of Jay, II, 48
27 William G. Sumner, History of American Currency, p. 55

accounting. Flour was not forwarded because there was no money
to pay the teamsters, but remained at the place of collection until
it spoiled. The cattle, which the states supplied for beef, were
allowed to wander away. Thus this experiment to carry on the
government without a medium of exchange was a complete failure.

In 1782, there was a ray of hope. Robert Morris, the able
Superintendent of Finance, recommended to Congress a plan for
funding the domestic debt and providing a means for its extinguishment.[28] Congress immediately passed a resolution to the effect that
if any surplus above the sum necessary to pay interest on the
national debt should arise from the funds granted by the states
for that purpose, it should form a sinking fund to be appropriated
to the payment of the principal of the national debt. But the
resolution was futile because neither state nor national finance
was in a condition to make a surplus possible.

Taxes were again assessed in 1783. By the middle of
1785 only one-fifth had been paid.[29] No one could suggest a
remedy for the state of things. Financial distress was widespread
and deepseated. Conditions were in marked contrast to 1775. At
the beginning of the war, the population was fairly prosperous
with its agriculture, its trade with England and the West Indies,
and its cod and whale fisheries. But the war had destroyed these

[28] William G. Sumner, Financier and Finances of the American Revolution.
[29] Albert S. Bolles, Financial History of the United States, p. 348

sources of revenue. Imports and exports stopped. England's navy kept us from the fisheries. Brissot de Warville, passing through New England at this time, spoke of the many idle men, the houses falling in ruins, miserable shops with scarcely anything in them, windows stuffed with rags -- all indicative of misery, the triumph of paper money and the influence of poor government.[30] By June 21, 1783, Congress had not a penny in the Treasury, with which to pay the army. The soldiers mutinied and the legislators were forced to flee to Princeton for safety.

Not only had Congress no currency to pay its obligations, but within the states themselves there was no money. In the absence of a circulatory medium, in most places barter came into use. Tobacco in Virginia and whiskey in North Carolina were used as measures of value. Isaiah Thomas, editor of the Worcester "Spy" announced that he would willingly receive subscription for his paper in salt pork.[31]

In 1788 there was a strong impetus to the issue of larger amounts of paper money. Debts by this time were high and printing paper was a quick method of paying them. Furthermore, the little specie left in the country was withdrawn on account of heavy imports. Not all states, however, participated in the currency issue. Despite strong agitation, Connecticut, New Hampshire,

[30] Brissot de Warville, _Travels in America,_ Ed. of 1794, I, 118
[31] Fiske, p. 165

- 14 -

Delaware, Maryland and Virginia refused to resort to the printing press.[32] Virginia, due mainly to the efforts of Madison, declared it "unjust, impolitic, destructive of public and private confidence, and of that virtue which is the basis of a Republican Government".[33] Instead, it decided that debts be paid in tobacco, or more specifically, "inspectors receipts, or notes for good merchantable crop tobacco".[34]The Rhode Island legislature, on the other hand, issued a series of Know Ye measures, commanding everyone to take paper money as equivalent for gold. The scrip was issued on the security of landed property of twice the value of the loan. It was to be legal tender. To refuse to take the money was an offense punishable by fine.[35] Creditors, knowing that the money would become worthless, closed their shops. Thereupon, business was at a standstill, except in barrooms. Farmers threw away their milk, used their corn for fuel, and let apples rot on the ground rather than supply the merchants. They threatened with armed violence, but finally surrendered when the merchants announced their intention of moving out of the state. These extraordinary proceedings incited disgust and alarm among sensible people in all the other states. Rhode Island was everywhere reviled. Since her form of certificates began with Know-Ye, the little state henceforth was called Rogue's Island -- the home of Know-Ye men and Know-Ye measures.

[32] Andrew McLaughlin, Confederation and the Constitution, p. 143
[33] Madison Writings, Hunt's Edition, II, 277 and 281
[34] Hening Statutes, XII, 258
[35] Frank G. Bates, Rhode Island and the Union, p. 125 and 126

In South Carolina, a powerful secret organization was formed called the "Hint Club".[36] Its purpose was to hint to certain people that they must accept paper money -- for houses were combustible and the use of firearms popular. Needless to say, no one dared refuse these fanatics. There were similar occurrences in Vermont and New Hampshire. But these disturbances were slight in comparison to those of Rhode Island.

In Massachusetts, the debtor class of the Western counties revolted under Captain Daniel Shays.[37] They closed the courts at Worcester and Concord and attacked the arsenal at Springfield. For five months the state was kept in terror. Finally, the insurgents were dispersed by the militia in a pitched battle at Petersham, February, 1787. Such incidents as this emphasized the confusion and distress rampant everywhere. Shays' rebellion, however, awakened the people to the dangers of political disunion. There was an immediate conservative reaction, which was a powerful aid to the formation of the Union.

The social upheaval was undoubtedly an expression of individualist sentiment, prevailing as a result of the revival of the philosophy of idealism. In a certain sense, people were capitalizing on disunion. Thomas Paine, writing of the speculators and debtors in 1786, said:

---

[36] Fiske, p. 169
[37] Andrew McF. Davis, Shays' Rebellion and the Political Aftermath, p. 24

> There are a set of men who go about making
> purchases upon credit and buying estates that
> they have not wherewithal to pay for; having
> done this, their next step is to fill the
> newspapers with paragraphs of the scarcity of
> money and the necessity of paper emission, then
> to have legal tender under the pretense of sup-
> porting its credit and when out to depreciate
> it as fast as they can, get a good deal of it
> for a little price and cheat their creditors;
> and this is the concise history of paper money
> schemes. 38

Knox, writing to Washington, thought that the trouble
was caused by uneasiness, a moral result of the Revolution:

> That taxes may be the ostensible cause is true,
> but that they are the true cause is as far
> remote from truth as light from darkness. The
> people who are the insurgents have never paid
> any or but very little taxes. But they see the
> weakness of the government: they feel at once
> their own poverty compared with the opulent
> and their own force, and they are determined to
> make use of the latter in order to remedy the
> former. 39

As for a consideration of banking during the revolutionary
period, there is no record of national or state banking before
1781. From 1775 to 1781 the country's finances were managed in
turn by treasurers, committees, and boards. In 1775, two treasurers
were appointed to receive and pay out public funds. That same
year, due to the inefficiency of the treasurers, a committee of
claims consisting of thirteen delegates, was appointed to
examine and report on all accounts against the government. The
following year the committee's number was reduced to five. In

38 Writings of Thomas Paine, II, 178
39 Brooks, Henry Knox, p. 194

1778 the system was again remodeled. A comptroller, auditor,
treasurer and two chambers of accounts were appointed only to be
superseded the next year by a Treasury Board.[40] The inefficiency
and laxity of the Board was incredible. It conducted its work with
such slowness as to preclude a successful administration. As
Hamilton said, "Its authority was divided. There was no unified
and responsible management".[41] Hence, in 1781, the Board was
replaced by a Superintendent of Finance. Morris' duty was to
examine into the public indebtedness, to review, digest and report
plans for improving and regulating finance, to establish order and
economy in the expenditures of public money, and to superintend and
control the settlement of all public accounts. This was the step
Hamilton had sought. In a letter to Robert Morris written in 1781,
he explicitly stated that the finances of the country should be in
the hands of a single man and that man should be Morris.[42]

Morris had great plans and ability. He hoped to
collect requisitions from states and to create a national income
from import duties which were to be paid in specie. Finally,
Morris desired to establish government credit through a bank.
He intended to make this the "principal pillar of American Credit,
so as to obtain the money of individuals for the benefit of the
Union and thereby bind those individuals more strongly to the

[40] Bolles, I, 91
[41] H.C. Lodge, Works of Alexander Hamilton, I, 220
[42] Ibid, p. 226

general cause by the ties of private interest"[43] Thus, on
May 26, 1781 the first bank (in the modern sense of the word) in
the United States was instituted. It was called the Bank of
North America. Its capitalization was to be $400,000 divided into
1000 shares at $400 each, payable in gold or silver.[44] The board
of twelve directors was to be chosen annually and would serve
without compensation. The bank would issue notes to the amount of
its capital stock. A daily report of the bank's condition had to
be made to the Superintendent of Finance.

Although the plan was sound, people hesitated to invest
in the enterprise. Morris had great difficulties in securing the
necessary subscription. By September 1, only $10,000 had been
subscribed.[45] After four months a French frigate brought $462,862
in silver, as a loan to the government. The entire amount was
deposited in the bank, but half was spent before the bank
opened. In its first few years, due to the heavy loans made to the
government, the Bank had very little money. After the war, however,
it enjoyed great prosperity, paying dividends of 14%.[46] The bank
had originally secured its charter from the state of Pennsylvania,
since doubt existed as to whether Congress had the power to
charter a bank. Soon complaints were made: a petition embodying
charges of favoritism, extortion, harshness to debtors, destruction

[43] John T. Holdsworth, Financing an Empire, Banking in Pennsylvania, p. 51
[44] Alva Konkle, Thomas Willing, the First American Financial System, p. 98
[45] Holdsworth, p. 32
[46] Lewis Lawrence, History of the Bank of North America, p. 15

of equality, led the legislature to rescind the charter in
September, 1785, only a few years after the Bank had rendered
inestimable service to the government. The Bank was forced
temporarily to secure a charter from Delaware until Pennsylvania,
fearing the loss of the valuable institution, renewed its charter
in 1787.[47]

There were two other banks founded in this decade: the
Bank of Massachusetts and the Bank of New York, both established
in 1784. Hamilton played a prominent role in forming the constitution and the policies of the Bank of New York. All three
institutions were sound precursors of Hamilton's later work.

A word must be said with respect to the work of Robert
Morris. Despite the tottering Articles of Confederation and the
delinquent Congress, Morris managed the country's finances compara-
tively well. Through his association with the Bank he secured
considerable loans from France, Spain and Holland. Occasionally
he had to resort to subterfuge. He frequently made a draft on
Franklin, in Paris, and then would discount it. He had no idea
from where the money would come. To give Franklin time to raise
the funds, Morris would take advantage of the poor methods of
communication which were then a feature of world finance. Knowing
that the business men of Cuba cleared their commercial paper

[47] See Thomas Paine's Dissertations on Government, Affairs of the
Bank, and Paper Money.

- 20 -

through Madrid, he would send a draft on Franklin to Cuba for
discount. The paper merchant who bought it would send it to the
banker in Madrid, and the latter would forward it to Paris.
Meanwhile, Morris would notify Franklin of the draft coming to
Paris through Havana and Madrid -- not knowing how or if Franklin
would be able to raise the money.[48]

Morris likewise indulged in many schemes and devices to
postpone payment of the government's debts. To prevent his being
constantly accosted by business men and importunate creditors,
he made Gouverneur Morris, Assistant Superintendent of Finance.
The latter was installed in a big, airy room on the third floor
of the Bank of North America. The numerous inquirers for Morris
would be ushered into Gouverneur Morris' office. There, beholding
a kindly gentleman with a wooden leg, not one would dare assault
him and all eventually were easily placated.

Morris, with the aid of the Bank of North America, managed
our finances well. It is to be regretted that he encountered
so much opposition. His own words best describe his predicament.

> Imagine the situation of a man who is to direct
> the finances of a country almost without revenue,
> surrounded by creditors whose distresses while
> they increase their clamors, render it more dif-
> ficult to appease them; an army ready to disband
> or mutiny; a government whose sole authority
> consists in the power of framing recommendations.[49]

[48] Theodore Grayson, Leaders and Periods of American Finance, p. 37
[49] Wharton's Diplomatic Correspondence of the Revolution, VI, 203

His principles were not those of the people and hence he resigned.
"To increase our debts while the prospect of paying them diminishes
does not consist with my idea of integrity. I must, therefore,
quit a situation which becomes utterly insupportable".[50] With
Morris' resignation in 1784 vanished all hope of straightening the
finances before 1789.

As Hamilton had several precedents for his banking
plans, so also, concerning mint and coinage, there was something
concrete on which to build. Robert Morris and Jefferson had
offered well-developed plans, but Congress was deaf to their pleas.
Yet the question required immediate action. A heterogeneous
collection of coins, with no uniform weight or value, was scattered
all over the states.[51] The value of money was differently regulated
by statute in every state. English, French, Spanish and German
coins of uncertain value passed from hand to hand. There were nine
pences, four pences, ha'-pennies, bits,[52] half-bits, pistareens,
picayunes,[53] and fips.[54] Of gold pieces, there were johannes, (joes)
doubloons, moidores, pistoles, English and French guineas, carolins,
ducats, and chequins. Of copper coins, there were English half-
pence, pence, French sous, and pennies issued from the local
mints in Massachusetts and Maryland. The English shilling was
universally used but had everywhere degenerated in value. In New

[50] Ibid, p. 229
[51] Neil Carothers, Fractional Money, p. 14
[52] Bit equals a Spanish real which equals $12\frac{1}{2}$¢; 2 reals equal 25¢
or 2 bits.
[53] Picayunes: so-called from small Spanish coin, picaillon.
[54] Fips: Pennsylvania's name for $\frac{1}{2}$ dime, Carothers, p. 35

England, 6 shillings equalled a dollar; in New York, 8 shillings;
in Georgia, 5 shillings; and in South Carolina, 32 shillings and
6 pence were equivalent to a dollar.[55] The Spanish milled dollar
had begun to supersede it as a measure of value.[56] This was due to
the fact that from 1776 the colonies had had favorable exchange
with the West Indies. Thus many Spanish coins circulated along-
side the English ones. Not only was this a serious obstacle to
trade, but it also served as an occasion for fraud and extortion.
Clipping and counterfeiting were carried on to such an extent
that every moderately cautious person in taking payments in hard
money, felt it necessary to keep a small scale beside him in order
to weigh each coin, after scrutinizing its stamp and attempting
to decipher its legend. The business of exchange was in a hopeless confusion. The American tables of exchange in 1786, with
their motley of dollars, shillings, moidores and pistareens, were
anything but pellucid. In addition, a half-dozen different kinds
of paper money created a condition which made exchange very
difficult. There is no wonder that men preferred to take whiskey
or pork. No one having a commodity to sell could tell how much
it was worth in money terms.

The Articles of Confederation gave Congress the exclusive
and sole power to regulate the alloy and value of coins circulating

---

[55] Report of Robert Morris, Superintendent of Finance, I, p. 289
[56] Bolles, II, 156

in the United States. In accordance with this prerogative, Congress in 1778 appointed a committee with Morris as chairman to
consider the state of money in the country. No further action
was taken until 1782 when the committee was instructed to prepare
for Congress a table of rates at which various foreign coins
should be received at the Treasury.[57] Morris took advantage of this
opportunity to set forth his reasons for establishing a national
coinage throughout the country.

On April 3, 1783, he submitted a comprehensive report of
the coinage system, pointing out the need of a uniform regulation.
He urged a silver standard, proposing a cent (1 cent), a quint
(5 cents) and a mark (10 cents), a coinage charge, and the decimal
system. He recommended the Spanish milled dollar as a monetary
unit and if a bimetallic standard should be adopted, suggested a
ratio of $14\frac{1}{2}$:1.[58] The plan threw considerable light upon a difficult
subject. Morris, with the aid of his assistant, Gouverneur Morris,
devised a system which would but slightly disturb the former value
of coins -- a system which was later to be of inestimable help to
Hamilton. Morris' accounts show that he also spent $2000 in
planning a mint. No coins were ever issued. Although the plans
met with approval, Congress took no action. The following year,
it referred the question to another committee of which Jefferson

[57] Journals of the Continental Congress, XXXVIII, 8
[58] Wharton's Diplomatic Correspondence, V, 103-110

was chairman. Jefferson's plan, submitted in July, 1785, was
similar to that of Morris, with the exception of the recommendation of a double standard and a greater variety of coins -- a
ten dollar gold coin, a silver dollar and dime, a twenty-cent
and a five cent piece, also a copper penny and half penny. He
suggested 15:1 for the ratio between silver and gold.[59] In July,
1785, Congress adopted three resolutions: that the money unit
of the United States be a dollar; that the smallest coin should be
a half-cent; and the coins to increase in value in decimal
ratio.[60] A year later an additional resolution was passed fixing
the fineness of gold and silver coins at 11/12ths (11 parts fine
to 1 part alloy) -- the unit (a dollar) to contain 375.64 grains
of fine silver. It provided for a mill as the lowest money of
account -- also a half cent, a cent, a ten-cent, a twenty-cent
and a half dollar coin, a ten dollar silver piece and a five and
ten dollar gold piece. The ratio between gold and silver was
estimated at 1:15.253.[61] The following month, an ordinance was
enacted establishing a mint and providing for silver and gold to be
coined at a ratio of 15:1. The legislation, however, was never
put into effect. Three or four dies were made for striking
copper coins, but no issue of coins ever took place.

The tariff laws of the revolutionary period were most

59 Henry R. Linderman, Money and Legal Tender in the United States, p. 21
(1887)
60 Journal of Continental Congress. Reprinted in Report of International
Monetary Conference, p. 448
61 D. R. Dewey, Financial History of the United States, p. 54

unsatisfactory. The colonial conditions were duplicated in an
exaggerated form. There was no national tariff. All attempts
of Congress to levy an import duty were unsuccessful. In 1781
Congress had requested permission to levy a 5% duty on foreign
imports.[62] Rhode Island and Virginia refused on the pretext that
it was a violation of their independence.[63] Inasmuch as the vote
for any legislation passed by the Congress of the Confederation
had to be unanimous, the bill was defeated. Two years later
another attempt was made to levy a duty on imported goods.
Congress asked the states for permission to levy a duty for twenty-
five years "as indispensably necessary to the restoration of
public credit".[64] But the states refused. It is difficult for us
to understand this attitude. With independence gained, one would
certainly think that the states would have united in common effort
to prevent English goods from flooding the American market and
from impairing the development of our manufactures. But independence
and victory did not mean union. Clashing interests, distrust,
suspicion and jealousy led each state to erect its own tariff
barrier. Consequently, instead of national legislation against
foreign competition, there came into existence a confused mass of
state legislation directed against sister states. From 1783 - 1788
New York taxed firewood from Connecticut and dairy products and

---

[62] Journal of Congress, February 3, 1781
[63] Staples, Rhode Island in the Continental Congress, p. 400
[64] Journals of Continental Congress. Reprinted in Report of International
Monetary Conference, I, 135

vegetables from New Jersey.[65] In turn, Connecticut suspended all
intercourse with New York. New Jersey, in retaliation, placed an
annual tax of $1800 on a light house built by New York on Sandy
Hook, New Jersey; Pennsylvania taxed tobacco from Maryland. Maryland
taxed whiskey from Pennsylvania. Virginia and Maryland argued constantly over the navigation of the Chesapeake Bay and the Potomac
River.[66] Massachusetts and Connecticut disputed over tolls levied
at the mouth of the Connecticut River on goods destined for
Springfield.[67] Besides the discriminating duties, there was fraud,
evasion and constant friction in trade. It was in an attempt to
allay these conditions that Hamilton had written the Continentalist
papers in 1781, advising a system of national protection. But
these essays had no immediate effect. In 1786, after several
attempts, he succeeded in calling the Annapolis Convention, attended
by representatives from Maryland, Virginia, New Jersey, Delaware
and Pennsylvania. The immediate outcome was the Philadelphia Convention and a Constitution for the United States.

 Currency, credit, banking, mint, coinage, tariff --
all imperatively demanded action. The state of our credit and
currency, however, was most in need of adjustment. As Washington
wrote to the Congress of the Confederation, "The great impediment
to all vigorous measures is the state of our currency -- I

---

[65] Fiske, p. 147
[66] Clark, p. 60
[67] Francis A. Walker, Making of a Nation, p. 2

- 27 -

should have little hope of the success of any project for raising
the value of currency, that can be adopted".[68] Had it not been
for a few hardy spirits like Morris, several times the government
would have foundered. "Public credit", according to H.T. Greene,
a member of Congress, "is so totally lost that private people
will not give their aid; though they see themselves involved in
one common ruin".[69]

Conditions were threatening to the maintenance of union.
The vast number of unfunded debts, the cumbrous load of useless
paper money, the loose system of bookkeeping led to confusion,
disorder, and corruption. Congressional activity was of a most
rudimentary character. From 1781 - 1789 experiments were tried,
but under the political circumstances were of little effect. Obligations of every variety were contracted without order or plan.
The financial system went from bad to worse, adversely affecting
our national credit. The efforts of Morris and Hamilton to fund
and consolidate the debt were of no avail. With foreign loans
unpaid, internal debts increasing, further loans impossible, and
requisitions unheeded, the outlook was decidedly dismal. The
matter of public accounting and financial report was especially
bad. Many of the public officials refused to furnish accounts of
money intrusted to them. There was diversion and transfer of funds.

68 Sparks, *Life of Washington,* I, 161
69 H.T. Greene, *Works of H.T. Greene,* I, 204

Negligence, wastefulness, disorder and corruption were rampant everywhere. Even in the darkest periods through which the country has since passed, it may be questioned whether a greater lack of system or moral rectitude prevailed. Adams writing to Jefferson (August 25, 1787) declared, "that all the perplexities, confusions and distress in America, rise not from the defects in their Constitution or Confederation, not from a want of honor or virtue, so much as from a downright ignorance of the nature of coin, credit and circulation".[70]

Few knew a solution. The financial system had to be renovated. But first it was necessary to change the political system. The states up to this point had no strong political ties, no sense of common interest and common destiny. Differences in race, language and religion served as obstacles to social, economic and political union -- and to a great degree were productive of distrust and animosity. With transportation and communication undeveloped, social intercourse was difficult.

The political organization was full of flaws. The war was based on the idea of personal right and liberty against authority. The Articles of Confederation reflected this philosophy. Congress was given negative powers. It could make laws, but not enforce them. It could tax the states, but could not compel payment. No

[70] John Adams, Works of John Adams, III, 447

effective legislation could be passed, since all resolutions,
except adjournment, had to be unanimous. The members of Congress
having so little power, took their responsibilities lightly. No
more than fifteen or twenty were ever present at meetings, although
that body was comprised of ninety-one members.[71] With the states
working at cross-purposes, following a policy of retaliation and
restriction instead of cooperation, it was necessary to destroy
the states as political entities.

In a certain sense, it was a blessing that the activities
of the weak central government and the states met with such vicis-
situdes. Gouveneur Morris' words contained a germ of truth.

> I will add, however, that I am glad to see
> things in their present train. Depend on it,
> good will arise from the situation, to which
> we are hastening -- although I think it pro-
> bable that much of convulsion will ensue, yet
> it must terminate in giving to the government
> that power, without which government is but a
> name.[72]

Washington proposed his remedy.

> It is clear to me as A B C, that an extension
> of federal powers would make us one of the
> most happy, wealthy, respectable, and powerful
> nations that ever inhabited the terrestrial
> globe -- I predict the worst consequences from
> a half-starved, limping government, always
> moving upon crutches and tottering at every
> step.[73]

Hamilton again and again expressed similar sentiments.
A strong, efficient central government was his objective. He

[71] Walker, The Making of a Nation, p. 14
[72] N. Sparks, Life of Gouveneur Morris, I, 249
[73] Fiske, p. 162

knew that the country would soon face bankruptcy and dissolution
if the states would not yield their powers to Congress. Hence,
he did all in his power to strengthen the central government.
With his oratory and powerful pen he helped persuade the states
to ratify the Constitution and thus paved the way for the union.
With an efficient central government it would be possible to
build a strong financial system. His words and plans materialized.
Within five years after the formation of the new government,
Hamilton, through his financial policies, laid the ground-work of
and gave the impetus to the financial and economic development of
the United States.

CHAPTER II

Origin and Development of Hamilton's Financial Ideas

When we reflect upon the chaotic financial condition of
the country in 1789, we wonder how Hamilton, at the age of thirty-
two, could have devised a financial system which today is still
in use. A brief consideration of his early career may be helpful
in an understanding of his later achievements. He had no special
training for finance. His early life involved a struggle amidst
poverty and social handicaps. His education was desultory.
However, while still young, he evidenced a precocity which led
the Rev. Hugh Knox, a clergyman and teacher in Nevis, to induce
the child's relatives to allow him to attend the school at
Christianstadt.[1] But the very next year, at the age of twelve,
due to strained financial circumstances, we find Hamilton working
at St. Croix for Nicholas Cruger, the leading merchant in the
Caribbean.[2] During the three years spent with Cruger, Hamilton
gave every indication of a grasp of business details. He was a
good trader, a keen forecaster, had an acute commercial sense, and
an excellent head for figures. At one time Cruger spent several
months in New York giving Hamilton, a stripling of fifteen, complete charge of his business. Letters written by Hamilton give
detailed methods of payment and specifications as to cargo and

[1] John T. Morse, Life of Alexander Hamilton, 2 Vols., Boston, Little,
Brown and Co., 1876, p. 10
[2] James Schouler, Alexander Hamilton, Small and Maynard Co., 1901, p. 14

disposition, which for clarity and logical precision are extraordinary.[3]

Although Hamilton spent little time at school, he received
from the Rev. Hugh Knox a classical education which is to be
envied. Such precocity, ingenuity, and resourcefulness did he
exhibit, that a collection was made among his relatives and friends
to send him to the States. After a year's preparation at Francis
Barker's Grammar School at Elizabethtown, New Jersey, he entered
King's College on his own plan -- a special student attached to no
class.[4] Latin, Greek, English, mathematics, chemistry and anatomy
were offered. Hamilton took all. He spent most of his time in
mathematics with his tutor, Dr. Herbert Harpur.[5] Animated by a
definite purpose, pursued with a steady and concentrated effort,
within two years he made unusual strides. At seventeen he
dedicated his pen to the cause of American independence and from
then on continued his work as a pamphleteer. A military career
interrupted but did not curtail his studies. As Washington's
aide, in spite of other duties, he found time to develop his
financial ideas. In his pay books, which he used for making notes,
we find entries which testify to his leanings towards the mastery
of the details of industry and trade. A few of these notations
may be cited. They indicate the interest of a lad of nineteen

3 Hamilton MSS, Library of Congress, I, 11
4 Henry J. Ford, Alexander Hamilton, Scribner's, 1920-p. 39
5 Robert I. Warshow, Alexander Hamilton, the First American Business
Man, Greenburg Publishing Co., 1931, p. 18

in finance.

> Trade with France greatly against Great Britain.
> Trade with Flanders in favor of Great Britain.
> Large balance in favor of Norway and Denmark.
>
> Aristotle's 'Politics', chapter 6, definition of
> money, etc.
>
> Proportion of gold and silver as settled by
> Sir Isaac Newton's proposition was 1:14. It was
> generally through Europe 1:15. In China, I
> believe it was 1:10.
>
> When native money is worth more than par in
> foreign, exchange is high, when worth less, it
> is low.
>
> Postlewait in his time supposes six millions
> of people in Great Britain. The ratio of increase
> has been found by a variety of observations to
> be that 100,000 people augment annually, one
> year with another -- (the rest is indistinct).
> Mr. Kerseboom agreeing with Dr. Halley, makes
> the number of people thirty-five times the number
> of births in a year.
>
> Dr. Halley's 'Table of Observations' exhibiting
> the probabilities of life containing an account
> of the whole number of people of Breslau, the
> capital of Silesia and the number of those of
> every age from 1-100. (The table follows).
>
> Postlethwaite supposes the quantity of cash
> necessary to carry on circulation in a state 1/3
> of the rents to the land proprietors or 1/6 of
> the whole product of the lands. (See articles
> Cash and Circulation).
>
> Money coined in Great Britain from the reign of
> Queen Elizabeth.[6]

6 Gertrude Atherton, The Conqueror, p. 148

In spare time, Hamilton worked on a synopsis of the
political and commercial history of Great Britain.[7] He was an
omnivorous reader. Among his papers we find long lists of books
of a most varied nature, ranging from classics to the novels of
the day. A list of references includes Hume, Smith, Socrates,
Cicero, Plato, Pliny, Plutarch, Shakespeare, Milton, Bacon,
Moliere, Voltaire, Diderot, Montaigne, Hobbes, Goldsmith, Gibbons,
Winn, and Ralb.[8]

While still in the army in 1780, he wrote Duane, a
member of the Continental Congress, his opinion as to how to
correct the defects of the government.[9] The two salient defects
mentioned were "want of power in Congress" and "lack of a method
and energy in administration". The letter is a brilliant exposi-
tion of the deficiencies of the Articles of Confederation.
Hamilton analyzed the reasons for the failure of Congress to cope
with the political situation. He described the struggle of the
Greek republics and the Swiss cantons in their attempts to form
a confederation without a strong central government. His advice
was "a solid coercive Union", and a "general convention summoned
immediately". Stress was placed on the central administration of
finance, for "that power which holds the purse-string absolutely
must rule". The great mistake in the Confederation was that it

[7] John C. Hamilton, Life of Alexander Hamilton, II, 23
[8] Allan McLane Hamilton, Intimate Life of Alexander Hamilton, Scribner's
and Sons, 1910, p. 32
[9] H.C. Lodge, Works of Alexander Hamilton, I, 229

gave the "power of the purse-strings too entirely to the state legislatures". An outline of the powers of the central government was included in the letter. The new Congress would have complete sovereignty in war, peace, trade and finance. It would regulate trade, impose taxes, lay prohibitions on articles of export and import, grant bounties and premiums, coin money, and establish a bank. Plans for the latter were given in great detail and will be considered under the section of the Report on the National Bank.

At twenty-three in two letters to Robert Morris, Hamilton constructively discussed the whole structure of the Confederation's financial affairs and practically laid the plan for the Bank of North America. In both letters a remarkable knowledge of finance is revealed. He modestly admitted that the plans were a product of "reading on the subjects of commerce and finance, and occasional reflections on our own particular situation".[10]

Upon leaving the army, Hamilton decided to study for the bar. Without a degree and without having had a formal law course, after four months of private study he passed the bar. Simultaneously he published a "Manual on the Practice of Law" which his friend Troup tells us "served as an instructive grammar to future students and became the ground-work of subsequently enlarged practical

[10] Lodge, III, 341

treatises".[11]

In 1782, Morris appointed Hamilton Receiver of Continental Taxes for New York. In this capacity he was earnestly responsive to inquiries from the Superintendent of Finance concerning supplies, taxes, fiscal conditions, etc. The Hamilton Manuscripts give an indication of the extent of his work. At a time when Morris was getting very little cooperation and information from his assistants, Hamilton deluged him with statistics. His work was interrupted after a half year, when he became a member of the Congress of the Confederation. About this time, Hamilton secured a copy of Adam Smith's "Wealth of Nations" and made an intensive study of the work, writing a commentary which unfortunately has been lost.[12] From 1783 - 1789, Hamilton worked excessively in an attempt to correct the defects of the government and to make the "changes necessary to save us from ruin".[13] The first few years were spent in persuading the "jarring, jealous and perverse" states to revise the Articles of Confederation. Mainly, through his efforts, a convention of six states was called at Annapolis in 1786. This in turn led to the Constitutional Convention of 1787. Here Hamilton displayed indefatigable zeal and unequalled enthusiasm. His work on the Federalist, wherein he convinced the States of the necessity of union, still stands as a classic on the American

[11] Atherton, p. 150
[12] Lodge, IV, 198
[13] Ibid, I, 47

constitutional system.

From this brief survey, it can readily be concluded
that Hamilton received no special training in finance. True, he
was an intense reader on financial subjects and was an interested
observer of financial legislation, but he had never actually
managed finances on a large scale. His manuscripts show that
through his relatives and friends he kept in constant touch with
financial developments in England and France and received the
latest publications from them.[14] A marked natural capacity,
remarkable vigor, resourcefulness, ingenuity, courage and a keen
business sense were probably his most marked equipment upon
entering a career as Secretary of the Treasury. He was a man
of action, possessing a deep mental insight and the courage of
his convictions. This likely accounts for the institution and
success of Hamilton's fiscal program. No part of it can be
attributed to originality, as he himself testified, or to
financial genius or phenomenal wizardry. It was the product of
deliberate study and of mature inquiry. Hamilton most carefully
observed the existing institutions in the leading European
countries, read and studied the works of economists, weighed
their theories, then put them into practice. The manner in

[14] Hamilton MSS, XI, 1157. Samuel Paterson from Edinburgh, Scotland
sent Hamilton four of the latest English publications: Price's State of
the Public Debt of Great Britain, Report of a Committee of Congress on
Income and Expenditure, Book of Rates, and Kearsley Tax Duties.
    II, 166, A letter from Chevalier Duplessis with promise to give
accounts of conditions, financial and economic, in France.
    V, Church, Hamilton's brother-in-law, kept Hamilton informed
as to the latest works and on many occasions sent copies of legal or
financial interest.

which these theories affected Hamilton's fiscal recommendations,
contained in his five reports, will be analyzed with a view as
to their originality, development and influence.

First and Second Reports on the Public Credit:-

Ten days after taking office as Secretary of the
Treasury, Hamilton was asked to submit to Congress a plan for
extricating the country from the difficulties in which its
credit and currencies were involved. The situation needed
complete reform. A debt of approximately 80,000,000 dollars,
consisting of foreign, domestic, state and unliquidated debts,
faced the nation. It was a staggering amount to handle, especially
since there was little precedent in the states as to the manner
of paying it. But Hamilton had read Dr. Price, Smith, and Hume.[15]
He was familiar with and kindly disposed towards the funding
system, the sinking fund, and the system of annuities and the
tontine as practiced in England. Accordingly, he utilized these
instruments of finance in his recommendations for extinguishing
the debt. The first Report on Public Credit, submitted on
January 14, 1790, marked the beginning of our financial system.
Hamilton, in writing the report, had only one objective. The
public credit of the nation must be unimpeachable. This could

15 Hamilton MSS, XI, 1157, XVII, 2295, XIII, 1775

result only from an effective provision for the existing debt.
The basic solution was to fund and consolidate all the national
debt and outstanding obligations of the United States and to
provide for their gradual payment over a period of years.[16] Even
though plans for funding the debt had been made in 1782 by Morris
and Hamilton,[17] with the approval of Congress and the sanction of
the states, yet, due to the political organization of the country,
it was impossible for plans to materialize. Now with the central
government being the "depository of the national interest",[18]
funding would be possible. Hamilton cited Great Britain as an
example where funding had been most frequently used. He added,
"It is remarkable that Great Britain -- the only power which has
uniformly cultivated an enlightened and excellent plan of national
credit -- continues to uphold the various branches of her commerce and industry in good energy and prosperity".[19] On the other
hand, France, not having made similar provision for her debt, was
thrown into the revolution by her financial embarrassments.
Funding the national debt would cement the states more closely
together and would promote security, order, confidence and
justice. It would benefit agriculture and commerce, since there
would be larger capital for their use, and it would lower the
interest rate, the latter always being in the ratio to the

[16] Lodge, II, 143
[17] John C. Hamilton, II, 15
[18] Federalist, No. 23, Bourne, I, 156
[19] Lodge, VIII, 446

quantity of money and the quickness of its circulation.

Following the discussion of funding, Hamilton next considered the nature, amount and provision for the national debt. The foreign debt, $10,070,307, with interest of $1,640,071, was to be paid according to the precise terms of the contract.[20] A loan of not more than $12,000,000 was authorized for payment of the foreign debt. This met with no objection. The domestic debt of $27,383, 917, plus interest of $13,030, 168, consisting of the loan office debt, army debt, marine debt, issues of quarter-masters and commissaries, the registered debt (certificates issued by the Register of the Treasury) and indents of interest (a species of paper payable to the bearer and issued on account of arrears of interest) was next considered.[21] Two thirds of the principal of the domestic debt would be funded in 6% stock, with interest from January 1, 1791 and one third in deferred 6%'s, interest beginning in 1800. The arrears of interest would be funded at full value in 3% stock with interest from July 1, 1791.[22] The question here was whether or not a discrimination between the original and actual holders of the debt should be made. The certificates of the domestic debt had so depreciated, that in 1789 they sold in the market for less than a quarter of their face value. Hamilton wanted them redeemed at their full

20 Ibid, II, pp. 254 and 236
21 Ibid.
22 American State Papers. Finance, I, pp. 26-37

value, with no discrimination.

Madison contended that this plan would yield a profit to the speculators and suggested, therefore, that the government pay the present holders what the certificates had cost them, plus the accrued interest since purchased, paying the balance to the original holders. Hamilton found this plan "replete with absurd as well as inequitable consequences", maintaining that it would be impossible to trace the original holders and perfectly just to neglect those who had so little faith in the credit of their government.[23] To make a discrimination between the original and present holders would be "unjust, impolitic, injurious and difficult" besides being a "breach of contract, -- a violation of the rights of a fair purchaser".[24] Furthermore, it proceeded upon a "principle destructive of the quality of the public debt, which is essential for its capacity for answering the purposes of money, that is, security of transfer".

The state debt, the principal and interest of which Hamilton calculated at approximately $25,000,000 would be assumed by the federal government. 6% interest upon 4/9ths of the debt would be given immediately; it would be deferred for ten years upon 2/9ths, and 3% allowed upon 3/9ths immediately. Assumption of the state debts would help to consolidate the

[23] Lodge, II, 234
[24] Ibid, II, 237

country's finances, and would give the government an effective
command of the Union's resources. It would further expedite
collection of revenue, attach the support of all creditors
to the interest of the union, and be "more orderly, better directed
and more uniform and comprehensive" than with thirteen different
systems.[25] Since most of the state debts had been incurred for the
general defense of the nation, Hamilton considered it only just
that the debts be assumed. He spoke of the contrary course being
followed in the provinces of the United Netherlands which resulted
in "perplexity and financial imbecility".[26]

     Another loan was to be opened for $10,000,000. For
every $100 subscribed (paid half in specie and half in debt) an
annuity of 5% would be given, irredeemable by any payment exceeding
$6.00 annually. The final loan proposed was on the principle of
a tontine.[27]

     To meet the interest and current service of the debt,
Hamilton advised increased duties on imports and tonnage. The
duties would affect only such luxuries as wines, spirits, teas
and coffee.

     Plans were made to institute a sinking fund. The revenue
of the post office, not exceeding $1,000,000, would be applied to
it annually. A commission consisting of the Vice-President, the

25 Hamilton MSS, IX, 22
26 Ibid, XIII, 1258
27 Lodge, II, 267

Speaker of the House, the Secretary of the Treasury and the Attorney-General would be entrusted with the management of the sinking fund.[28] The commissioners were to borrow $12,000,000 for payment of the interest and installments on the foreign debt to supplement any deficiency which might occur in the revenue to be applied to the interest of the domestic debt and for purchase of the public debt at the market price, if below par.

The foregoing propositions were the means to attain the objective "the firm establishment of public credit". Hamilton believed that "the character, security and prosperity of the nation" depended on the adoption of his fiscal program.[29]

In the second Report on the Public Credit presented on January 15, 1795, a resume was made of the revenues established, of the provisions for funding the debt and paying interest on it and of redeeming and reimbursing the public debt. Duties on import, tonnage of ships, distilled spirits, postage of letters, fees on patents, dividends on the bank stock, duties on snuff, refined sugars, sales at auctions, carriages and licenses to retail wines and distilled spirits -- had been imposed for revenue.[30] The first three were pledged to payment of interest on the public debt; the others, for current service of the debt. The Act of August 4, 1790 instituted a sinking fund, appropriating to it

[28] Ibid, p. 282
[29] Ibid, p. 281
[30] Ibid, III, pp 202-210

the proceeds from the sales of the western lands.[31] The surplus of
duties on imports and tonnage were to be applied to the sinking
fund. A commission was established to manage the fund and to buy
government stock at or below par. The legislation of May 8, 1792,
established a permanent sinking fund, composed of interest on
the public debt purchased, redeemed, or paid into the Treasury
in satisfaction of any debt or demand and the surplus of moneys
appropriated for paying interest on the public debt.

After a thorough survey of what had been accomplished
by funding the debt and instituting a sinking fund, Hamilton
concluded that an attempt should be made and was possible, to pay
the debt foreign and domestic in a period "not exceeding thirty
years."[32] Furthermore, payment of the debt should be under the
"direction of the commissioners" who were to fix its destination
by "faithful application" of the funds intended for it.[33] He
maintained that an "inviolable application of an adequate sinking
fund is the only practicable security against an excessive
accumulation of debt, and the essential basis of a permanent
national credit."

The two reports, the first, containing Hamilton's
fiscal policies before their application, and the second, a review

[31] Ibid, p. 216
[32] Ibid, pp. 236 and 265
[33] Ibid, p. 266

of them after their institution, are the classical indices to the formation of the financial policies of the nation. Hamilton in preparation had labored intensely. His manuscripts include references to the following important English publications:

      Price, Richard, The State of the Public Debt of Great Britain.
      Anderson, Adam, Annals of Commerce.
      Book of Rates of Customs and Valuations. Scotland Laws, Statutes, etc., 1567 - 1625.
      Report of a Select Committee of the House of Commons on Income and Expenditures. 1786.
      Kearsley Tax Duties which Contain the Inland and Excise Duties.[34]

No direct quotation from any of these sources is included in either report. It may be possible that Hamilton had not read them, but had noted them as possible references for future use. Yet, in view of the fact that previous to his incumbency, as Secretary of the Treasury, he had little training in finance, we can only conclude that he availed himself of much material through the aforementioned works.

Hamilton's recommendations for funding the debt, for the use of the sinking fund, annuities and the tontine were new expedients. Although the latter two proposals were not accepted, they indicate, nevertheless, acquaintance with the very latest and the most intricate of financial devices. In a consideration of the origin and development of Hamilton's fiscal policies, it

[34] Hamilton MSS, IX, 1157

will be necessary to review briefly the history of these instruments of finance. The annuity was a yearly or periodic payment
of a certain sum of money granted to one for life, for years or
in fee chargeable on the person of the grantor. From the 11th to
the 15th century the expenses of petty wars in Italy, Germany and
England were met by loans repayable as annuities. Calculations
were mere guesswork until the work of Jan de Witt, who based his
computations on the mortality experience of the 17th century.
Hamilton had studied the use of annuities in English finance. In
funding the debt he thought "the whole system of annuities as
practiced in England may be ingrafted upon it".[35] He used Halley's
tables for computing his annuities.[36] Two types were offered:
annuities certain -- payment made at equal intervals over a period
of years, and annuities contingent -- payment depending on the
happening of some event. The desirable feature of the annuity was
that the government would have to pay a rate of interest of 4% only.
There were to be four classes. $100 advanced upon the life of an
eleven year old person would produce an annuity of:

```
$10,346 if payments commenced at 21
 18.803    "       "          "   " 31
 37.286    "       "          "   " 41
 78.580    "       "          "   " 51. [37]
```

$100 advanced upon the chance of survivorship of the

[35] Lodge, III, 339
[36] Ibid, II, 291
[37] Ibid, p. 267

younger of two lives, one being twenty-five and the other thirty, would produce, if the younger should survive, an annuity for the remainder of his life of $23.55.

As an "auxiliary expedient and by way of experiment", an elaborate plan for a tontine was suggested.[38] The tontine was a sort of pseudo-annuity. It was used by Mazarin and Colbert to resuscitate French finances. The plan was originated by Lorenzo Tonti, a Neapolitan banker and financial adviser to Mazarin.[39] Tonti's proposition called for a sum of 25,000,000 pounds to be collected each year and interest paid on it at a lower rate to the younger and at a higher rate to the older members. Individual subscriptions were to be 300 pounds. The subscribers were divided into ten age classes, each constituting a closed group. The surviving members of each class received annually a pro-rata share of the interest fund allotted to each class. After the death of the last member, the original fund reverted to the state. At first the tontine was not so successful. The public did not understand its operation and consequently hesitated to invest in the enterprise. The merits of the first tontine could not be determined, due to its short life. In 1689 Pontchartrain resuscitated the idea and offered a tontine with an interest rate of 5% to the younger and $12\frac{1}{2}$% to the older members.[40] The sub-

---

[38] Ibid, II, 267
[39] Jacques Moulin, Des Tontines, p. 3
[40] Ibid, p. 8

scribers were divided into fourteen classes, each subscriber
giving 300 pounds. On this occasion the tontine was a great
success, and in a short time was over-subscribed. It ended in
1726. Attempts were made in 1696, 1709, 1733 and 1744 to use
the tontine again, but unsuccessfully. In 1785, the first private
tontine was authorized by letters of patent from King Louis XVI
to his cousin, the Duke of Orleans.[41] Ten years later it was taken
over by the state. The English had utilized the tontine to help
pay the expenses of the Revolutionary War. Hamilton's tontine
was based on that introduced by Pitt a few months before Hamilton
took office. It is obvious that he took advantage of the
freshest expedient.

The proposed tontine was to consist of six classes,
composed of persons of the following age:

20 and under:	the annuity upon a share in the	first	class	to be	$8.40
20 - 30:	" " " " " " "	second	"	" "	8.65
30 - 40:	" " " " " " "	third			9.00
40 - 50:	" " " " " " "	fourth	"	" "	9.65
50 - 60:	" " " " " " "	fifth	"	" "	10.70
60 and above:	" " " " " " "	sixth	"	" "	12.80 [42]

Each share would be $200 and the numbers of shares in each class
would be indefinite. The annuities of those who died were to be
divided among the survivors until 4/5ths were dead, when the
principle of survivorship was to cease and each annuitant thence-
forth would enjoy his dividend as a several annuity during the life

[41] Ibid, p. 16
[42] Lodge, II, 267

upon which it depended. Annuities were to be calculated on the
longest life of each class at the rate of 4%. A tontine on a
similar basis was successful abroad and for that reason an
attempt was made to introduce it into the United States. But
Congress, not understanding the intricacy of the proposition,
hesitated to adopt it.

In order to expedite the funding of the debt, a sinking
fund was proposed.[43] Hamilton's main argument in favor of the
sinking fund was that the debt when funded became stable and
suitable for investment. The Dutch had first used the sinking
fund in 1655, when the interest on the national debt was reduced from 5% to 4% and the 1% saved was employed to discharge
the debt.[44] The English had had a century of experience with this
form of debt retirement. The plan achieved prominence after
1688 owing to the increase of the public debt after the wars of
William of Orange. The first sinking fund in England was established
in 1713 after the Treaty of Utrecht. Subsequently, Britain
created three sinking funds: the Aggregate, the General, and the
South Sea Funds -- the revenues of which were attached to the
interest of the public debt. The fourth sinking fund was put
into operation by Walpole. It was called the Stanhope Sinking
Fund after Lord Stanhope, a member of Parliament, who introduced

43 Ibid, II, 282
44 A. Anderson, Annals of Commerce, II, 575

the bill providing for its institution.[45] To this were appropriated the surpluses remaining after the charges of the other three funds had been satisfied. This was to be a group of revenues exclusively applied to the principal of the public debt and definitely derived from the budget surplus. It was cumulative, since as the debt was retired, the surplus of the three funds increased. The surplus of certain specific duties and funds was to be appropriated, reserved and employed for discharging the principal and interest of the national debt. These annual savings were to be invested and eventually the accumulated money would pay off the previously incurred debt. Sir Nathan Gould in his Essay on the Public Debt of the Kingdom, published in 1726, had put forth the sinking fund theory. Walpole followed Gould's plan but was unsuccessful in carrying it out. Genuine surpluses were not applied to the debt, but were diverted from their original purpose. However, the continuing increase of the public debt as a result of frequent wars, maintained public interest in the efficacy of debt retirement.

In 1772, with great force and persuasion, Dr. Price published his Appeal to the Public on the Subject of the National Debt , wherein he proposed a new plan for the sinking fund. Interest alone was to be applied to the public debt.[46] Price held that this

[45] N.A. Brisco, Economic Policy of R. Walpole, p. 40
See also: Lecky, History of England in the 18th Century, I, 320
Robert Hamilton, Public Debt, p. 135
McCulloch, Taxation, p. 476
[46] Ibid, p. 2

kind of sinking fund, be its income ever so much exceeded by new
demands, incurred annually, would soon become superior to them
and cancel them. Thus the state may without difficulty redeem
all its debts by borrowing money for payments into the sinking
fund. The plan involved a permanent annual sinking fund to be
used to buy the public debt. The debt was to be kept alive by the
continuation of interest payments to the sinking fund and these
interest payments were to be used for the purchase of the public
debt. The "magic wand" of compound interest would gradually reduce
the debt even though the initial fund was small. Price spoke of
the amazing increase of money bearing compound interest. He
emphasized the fact that the

> duration of lives of individuals is confined
> within limits so narrow as not to admit in any
> great degree of the advantages that may be
> derived from the increase. But a period of
> 50 or 60 or 100 years, being little in the
> duration of kingdoms, they are capable of
> securing them in almost any degree. 47

The sinking fund would absorb any debt if maintained inviolate and
if annual payments were made to it. For the latter, it would be
well to borrow since the government would borrow at simple interest
and invest in its stock at compound interest. As an example of the
efficacy of a sinking fund, Price gave the following: a penny put
out at 5% compound interest in the year I, would in 1775 amount to
300,000,000 millions of earths all solid gold.[48] At simple interest

47 Richard Price, Appeal to the Public on the Subject of the National Debt.
48 Ibid, p. 38

it would amount to only 7 shillings and 6 pence.

The Price plan was put into operation in 1786 by Pitt, by combining the revenues attached to the four funds into a "consolidation" fund. In order to keep the sinking fund intact, Pitt placed it under the supervision of a special Board of Commissioners of the Sinking Fund.[49] The Board would purchase public stock quarterly at or below par. Unfortunately, the plan was not a success in spite of all the precautions. At first the interest was paid on the debt from the budget surplus, but gradually undue optimism led to laxity in annual appropriations which in turn led to deficits in the sinking fund. Furthermore, after 1793, the financial strain of the war with France made a surplus impossible.

Hamilton, having read from Hume and Price, and being an admirer of Pitt, introduced the sinking fund. He was aware of its pitfalls, but was determined to escape them. As before mentioned, he insisted on the inviolable application of the proceeds from the sale of Western lands. Also, the interest of so much of the debt as had heretofore been redeemed was pledged to the sinking fund. A special commission consisting of the Vice-President, Chief Justice, Secretary of the Treasury, Secretary of State, and Attorney-General was authorized to make purchases for the fund and render appropriate accounts (May 8, 1792). The

[49] Edward Ross, Sinking Funds, VII, 324. Publicationsof American Economics Association.

surplus of all duties on imports, tonnage and liquors after satisfactory prior appropriations, were to be applied to the sinking
fund. The net product of the post-office not exceeding $1,000,000
was vested in the commission to be applied to discharging the public
debt by purchase of stock in the market or by payments on
account of the principal.[50] In 1795, the powers of the commission
were enlarged. This sinking fund, though inspired by English example,
was managed more carefully and conservatively than the English fund.
Hamilton, convinced of its value both in theory and practice, was
insistent upon various restrictions on its character and faithful
appropriations of specific revenues.

Progress in extinguishing the debt, however, was slow.
Interest was promptly paid from revenues derived from taxation
and from the proceeds of loans authorized for the purpose. But,
on the other hand, the debt bequeathed by the former government's expenditures was increased in consequence of the Indian
War, the Whiskey Insurrection, the Barbary difficulties, the
aggressions of France, and the Louisiana Purchase.[51] By 1832,
however, due in great part to Hamilton's plans and principles,
the debt was paid.[52] The details of Hamilton's funding program
may be criticized, yet the measures meet the test of sound practice.
They were not original -- they were almost slavishly imitative

[50] Hamilton MSS, XXIV, 3274
[51] D.B. Dewey, Financial History of the United States
[52] Jonathan Eliot, Funding System of the United States and Great
Britain, p. 223

of the English system. Hamilton showed no effort to invent
theories leading to novel expedients. He sought, rather, to
adopt methods and agencies which had been tested by experience.
He seldom showed a disposition to go beyond the range of
experiments already tried. The matter was really too grave and
the consequences too important to permit of experiment. The only
valuable guides were England and Holland. France was in the midst
of a revolution, partly a result of poor financing. Spain had lost
her opportunities and resources. Russia and Austria were struggling
with inconvertible paper and financial distress. England was the
logical example.

Perhaps the funding act was too complicated as a piece
of fiscal workmanship. It created a variety of new stocks and
bonds with varying interest rates and varying terms of redemption.
It was difficult to picture clearly the fiscal conditions of the
government from year to year. The error undoubtedly lay in
giving too long a life to the new obligations. On the whole,
however, funding in the United States served its purpose. It did
not operate as Jefferson intimated, for the "purpose of mystifying
the public and establishing a perpetual debt." Funding was instituted because it was the only alternative, other than repudiation.

Report on the National Bank:-

Hamilton's second report, presented to Congress on December 13, 1790, concerned a national bank. The report was the result of ten years of study of the banking systems of Europe. For fully a decade, Hamilton had regarded a national bank as an "indispensable engine in the administration of the finances of the country." [53]

At the age of twenty-three in a letter to Duane (September 3, 1780) Hamilton discussed the state of the country's credit. At this early date, there was no bank in the United States. Congress was blocked because it had no source of funds to meet its expenses. Hamilton recommended a bank founded on public and private credit. "The Bank of England," he asserted, "unites public authority and faith with private credit, and hence we see what a vast fabric of public credit is raised on a visionary basis."[54] He contended that the paper money of the country had depreciated because "moneyed men had not an immediate interest to uphold its credit." It was necessary to get the moneyed men interested in banking and to engage in it as a business. The plan for a bank given in the letter to Duane, was very sketchy, inasmuch as Hamilton was immediately concerned with the political situation, rather than with the economic.

It is necessary, however, to mention the salient points

[53] Lodge, III, 391
[54] Ibid, I, 234

of the outline. The Bank's capital would be 1,000,000 pounds.
One-fourth of this was to be in specie, three-fourths in real
property. The Bank would issue notes to the extent of its stock.
Loans to the government would be made at 6%, to the public at 8%.
The Bank would purchase government annuities as was done in England.[55]
This letter to Duane, although of no immediate influence, contained
the germ of later plans.

In a letter to Robert Morris, written in 1780, Hamilton
repeated his advice as to the establishment of a national bank.
He was adamant in his contention that the only plan which could
preserve the country was one which would "make it the immediate
interest of the moneyed men to cooperate with the government in its
support."[56] He likened our condition to that of France. There paper
money had dwindled to almost nothing. Efforts of the government to
revive it were of no avail, since the people had lost confidence
in it. Law brought forth a plan which united the interest and
credit of the rich with the state. He founded a bank modeled on
the Bank of England. The foundation was good, but unfortunately
the superstructure was too great. Hamilton realized this,
advising "take what is good in this plan and others avoiding their
defects and excesses."[57] He laid out his plan carefully. The
institution chartered for ten years was to be called the Bank of

55   Ibid, pp. 235,236,237
56   Ibid, III, 332
57   Ibid, p. 333

the United States. Its capital would be only $2,000,000. It
would lend to the government at 4%, but to the public at 6%. The
government was to share one-half of the stock and profits of the
Bank. The Bank, managed by trustees, would be inspected by a Board
of Trade who would have recourse to the Bank's books. This was the
"practice in England and in other countries where banks are
established."[58]

In the second letter to Morris, written the following year,
Hamilton spoke of the Bank as being a source of national strength
and wealth.[59] He enumerated the accomplishments of the banks of
Genoa, Venice, Hamburg, Holland and England. He cited the example
of the Bank of England which was instituted when, due to the wars
of King William, the country had been drained of its specie, its
commerce and revenues had decreased, and taxes were no longer productive. The Bank relieved these national difficulties. The
United States at this time having no revenue, no credit and no
specie, it would be necessary to have recourse to a national bank
in order to institute a wholesome, solid and beneficial credit.
The plan here submitted was more detailed than the one suggested
previously, but in essentials it was the same. The Bank's capital
would be 3,000,000 pounds divided into shares. Notes would be
issued payable at sight in pounds, shillings and pence. The

58 Ibid, p. 335
59 Ibid, p. 342

interest rate on loans could not be higher than 8%. The stock
was to be subscribed for, all in specie if only 5 shares; one-half
in specie, and one half in landed security if from 6-15 shares;
two-sixths in specie, one-sixth in bills of security and good
European funds and three-sixths in good landed security if above
15 shares. Foreigners would be allowed to subscribe.[60] Many of
Hamilton's suggestions were incorporated in the Bank of North
America established in 1781. Morris himself testified to this in
writing to Hamilton, "I not only think, but on all proper occasions
shall say that the public are indebted to you for this plan."[61]

In 1784, Chancellor Livingston proposed a land bank for
New York City.[62] Its capitalization was to be $750,000 one-half
to be paid in cash and two-thirds in land security. Hamilton
now objected to the land security feature, since most of the
colonial issues which had failed to be redeemed were based on
land. Consequently, he submitted a proposition for a bank based
on gold and silver specie only. The plan met with approval and
Hamilton was asked to write the Constitution of the Bank of New
York. The Bank's capitalization would extend from $500,000 to
$1,000,000.[63] There were to be thirteen directors. Each
shareholder would have one vote. The principle of decrease of
voting power with increase of holdings was put into effect. The

---

60 Ibid, p. 367-380
61 Dip. Corresp. Rev., IX, 336
62 Hamilton MSS, VI, 695
63 Allen Nevins, History of the Bank of New York and Trust Company, p. 3

Bank could discount notes and bills at 6% a year. Debts could
not exceed the capital subscription to the bank; no property
could be held, except that necessary to the purposes of banking.
The Bank was not allowed to buy or sell stock. For two years,
Hamilton was director of the Bank of New York.[64] Thereafter, he
kept in constant touch with the activities of the Bank.

The above details throw some light on the early development of Hamilton's banking principles. It is striking that in
1780 Hamilton proposed a land bank and four years later refused
to accept one. The intervening political and economic development convinced Hamilton that land, because of its fluctuating
value, was a poor security. A more stable value was necessary.
Besides this, there was little change in Hamilton's essential
ideas.

The Hamilton Manuscripts contain little material on
the preparation of the Report on the National Bank. One of two
conclusions can be drawn. Hamilton having discussed banks for
a decade, offering several plans, and having personal experience
with the Bank of New York, knew what he wanted. It was not
necessary to make investigations. They had been made as early
as 1780. The Report on the National Bank was to be based entirely
on his former plans, modified by experience and circumstances.

[64] Ibid, p. 3

On the other hand, no one knows how much of the Bank Report material was contained in the Bank building and was burned during the conflagration of 1814.

It is obvious, however, from Hamilton's early letters, and from the Report itself, that he paid special attention to the Bank of England. Perhaps his staunch devotion to the English system of government induced him to study the English system of economy so faithfully. The many references to the Bank of England demand that we make at least a few descriptive remarks about that institution.

The Bank of England grew out of a loan of 1,200,000 pounds to the government. In addition, 300,000 pounds were to be raised by subscription, the subscribers to receive annuities. For the total 1,500,000 pounds, duties on the tonnage of ships, beer, ale, and liquors were pledged. The Bank could deal in bills of exchange, gold and silver bullion. Debts could not exceed the Bank's capitalization, otherwise the stockholders would be liable in proportion to the amount of stock held. The twenty-four directors had to be inhabitants of England.[65]

In the Report, Hamilton explained fully why it was necessary to organize a new banking institution for the United States. It was impossible to use the Bank of North America. The

[65] Joseph Francis, Bank of England, p. 16

latter was under a state charter and thus subject to state
politics. Besides, its capitalization, now only two millions,
"rendered the institution an incompetent basis for the extensive
purposes of a national bank." [66]

There was only one bank for Hamilton to use as a model --
the Bank of England. The French Caisse d'Escompte was embarrassed
by its close connections with the government. It could not conceal
the inconvertibility of its paper money. The Bank of Amsterdam
was of little use as a pattern, being organized upon a plan adopted
for an opulent community, rich in specie, and indifferent to the
use of bank credit. It was a bank of deposit only, and not of
loan or issue, hence, "less useful".[67] The Bank of England, on the
other hand, was a paragon of financial stability. It was a most
successful institution, strengthening private enterprise, aiding
the government with its fiscal policies, and regulating currency
on a sound basis.

Having established the importance of banking in European
countries, Hamilton drew up his plan, which was adopted without
modification by Congress. To convince the doubtful members of
Congress of its validity, he gave a detailed account of its
advantages. It would facilitate the government's fiscal operations
and would establish a broader and stronger credit and currency

[66] Lodge, III, 416
[67] Ibid, p. 429

system for the entire country, thus promoting uniformity in these
important matters. Through its lending powers, it would increase
the amount of capital available for the development of natural
resources and the encouragement of manufactures; stimulate business
by serving as a central exchange office for investment opportunities;
furnish the government with a convenient fiscal agent for the
negotiation of loans, payment of interest on the public debt, and
for the deposit of Treasury balances. Finally, it would have a
monopoly in carrying out the details of Federal finances, would
help the government lay and collect taxes, borrow money and
regulate trade, currency and national defense. Then followed
Hamilton's detailed outline of the Bank -- strikingly similar
in its management, powers, scope, redemption of notes and debt
limitations to the Bank of England. The institution was to be
chartered for twenty years, sufficient time "to judge of its
advantages or disadvantages".[68] Its capital stock was to be
$10,000,000. This would enable the "erection of a capital
sufficiently large to be a basis of extensive circulation." The
stock would be divided into 25,000 shares at $400 each, payable
1/4 in gold and silver coin, and 3/4 in 6% government stock.
Hamilton thought it would be impracticable to collect all
this in metal, for since the debt comprised part of the capital,

[68] Ibid, pp. 390-395

it should be used as such. Besides, in "enabling the Bank to
extend its operations and, consequently, enlarging its profits, it
would produce a revenue of 6% annually."[69] Conversions of the
public debt into bank stock would also "accelerate its rise to
the proper point." The final argument in favor of the fitness
of the public debt for the bank fund was the fact that "the
Bank of England rested wholly on that foundation."[70]

Due to unfavorable experience on the part of the Bank
of North America, the Bank of the United States would be limited
in its real estate holdings.[71] It could, however, hold such
property as it needed for its accommodation, or which was
mortgaged to it by way of security or conveyed in satisfaction
of debts contracted in the course of its dealings.

The total indebtedness of the Bank was not to exceed
its capital stock. This restriction did not exist in the Bank of
North America, but did exist in the Bank of England. "As a
source of security, it was worthy of imitation."[72] In case of an
excess of loans, the directors would be personally liable as
were the directors in the Bank of England.

The Company or Bank could sell public stock, but could
buy nothing except bills of exchange, gold and silver bullion
(another restriction found in the charter of the Bank of England).

69 Ibid, p. 438
70 Ibid, pp. 438,439
71 Ibid, pp. 438,432
72 Ibid, p. 439

Hamilton feared that the Bank's buying of public stock might lead to speculation.

No more than 6% could be charged on the Bank's loans or discounts. This interest rate limitation was dictated by the "consideration of different rates prevailing in different parts of the Union and as the operations of the Bank may extend through the whole, some rule seems to be necessary."[73] Furthermore, Hamilton believed that a low rate of interest would stimulate trade and industry.

No loan could be made in excess of $100,000 to a state government, unless previously authorized by special legislation; under no circumstances could a loan be made to a foreign state or prince. This would serve as a "barrier to executive encroachments and to combinations inauspicious to the safety or contrary to the policy of the United States."

The management of the Bank would consist of twenty-five directors, who were citizens of the United States, elected by the stockholders according to a plan which gave the small holder relatively more votes in proportion to their shares than the large ones. Hamilton feared "that a few might" monopolize the power and benefits of the bank.[74] Not more than three-fourths of the directors, therefore, could be reelected in successive years, since it was desirable to "have a principle of rotation -- for

73 Ibid, p. 440
74 Ibid, p. 423

by lessening the danger of combinations among directors to make
the institution subservient to party rules, or to the accommodations of any particular set of men, it will render the public
confidence more stable."[75] As a precaution against foreign
influence, no foreign stockholders were eligible as directors,
nor were they permitted to vote, even by proxy.

The Bank was required to make a statement of its condition to the Secretary of the Treasury, for Hamilton thought that
the Government should see that "so delicate a trust be executed
with care and fidelity."[76] This was also the practice in England
and other European countries.

The President was to authorize a subscription of
$2,000,000 to be made by the government to the stock of the Bank.
This was done in order to enlarge the specie fund of the Bank and
to enable it to initiate its activities sooner. "Though it is
said to borrow with one hand what is lent with the other, yet the
disbursement of what is borrowed will be progressive and bank
notes may be thrown into circulation instead of gold and silver."
To this he added the consideration that "as far as the dividend
of the stock shall exceed the interest paid on the loan, there is
a positive profit."[77]

From the foregoing account, it is obvious that the first

[75] Ibid, p. 422
[76] Ibid, p. 431
[77] Ibid, p. 438

Bank of the United States was modeled almost exclusively on the Bank of England. In fact, all of Hamilton's plans for a bank, in 1780 (in the letter to Duane), 1781 and 1782 (in the letters to Robert Morris) and 1784 (the Bank of New York) had essentially the same structure, differing only in details. Upon concluding his outline in the Report, Hamilton aptly remarked: "The Bank of England rested wholly on this foundation."[78]

It is not necessary to say that the institution of the Bank of the United States was a success. The fact that the bank stock was over subscribed within two hours indicates that the whole plan met with approval.[79] Maclay, in the Senate, expressed the current feeling: "that it is totally in vain to oppose the bill."[80]

The Bank proposal met with objections from Jefferson and Randolph, but Hamilton's elaborate defense nullified their dissent. Randolph objected to the bill on the ground that the Constitution did not give Congress power to create corporations. Jefferson argued that the Bank was neither necessary nor proper for carrying out the powers given to Congress. Hamilton answered the objection, insisting that the principle of incorporation is "inherent in the very definition of government" and proving that the Bank was a necessary and proper agency in such important duties as laying and collecting taxes, borrowing money, regulating currency and trade

---

78 Ibid.,p. 439
79 George Gibbs, Administrations of Washington and Adams, p. 68
80 William Maclay, Journal of 1789-1791, p. 69

and national defense.[81] It is in this dispute that Hamilton
was the first to evoke the argument in favor of the implied
powers of the Constitution, thus establishing an important
precedent.

A few months after the bank stock was on the market,
it was selling at a premium of 40 points.[82] In eighteen years
its average dividend was $8\frac{1}{2}$%.[83] All during its life, the Bank
was wisely and conservatively managed, performing its functions
well during its twenty years' existence.

Report on Mint and Coinage:-

The next contribution was our mint and coinage system.
Hamilton's extensive report was presented to Congress on January
28, 1791.[84] Despite the variety of considerations involved in
the subject, he fully comprehended the importance of the inquiry.
He made an exhaustive investigation into the nature of the monetary
unit, the ratio between gold and silver, the proportion and composi-
tion of alloy in each kind, whether the expense of coinage should
be defrayed by the government, the number, size, denomination and
devices of coins, what steps should be taken concerning foreign
coins, whether they should be allowed to pass current or not, and
if so, at what rate.

81 Ibid, III, P. 446
82 J. T. Holdsworth, Financing an Empire, p. 82
83 Life and Correspondence of Rufus King, I, p. 402
84 Lodge, IV, 3

But here there was little need for originality. Hamilton

had a number of suggestions and experiments from which to select.

Nevertheless, in the Hamilton Manuscripts the following books are

listed:

Arbuthnot, John: Table of Ancient Coins, Weights and
Measures, 1727
Newton, Sir Isaac: Table of Assays, Weights and Values
of Most Foreign Silver and Gold Coins, London, 1740.
Kruse, Jurgen Elert: Allgemeiner und besondere hamburgischer
contorist, Hamburg, 1771-72.
The British Negotiator or Foreign Exchange made Perfectly
Easy, Slack, Thomas (S. Thomas, pseud.), London. J. Richardson, 1759?
Leslie's Improvement of the Proposition of Hatton and
Whitehurst, 1747
Parairi, J: Modern Universal Tables of the Monnies,
Weights and Measures of the World. (translated into English), Dublin, 1756.
Representations of the Merchants of Amsterdam respecting
Gold Coins, 1750.
Tableau du Pair des Monnies et des Changes des Principales
Villes de l'Europe. Poids ou Marc d'Or et d'Argent. Paris, 1757. [85]

These references indicate the fact that Hamilton thorough-

ly studied the coinage systems of Europe, even though he based his

recommendations almost entirely on those previously made and adopted

by the Continental Congress.

As early as 1775, the Continental Congress had selected

the unit, when it authorized an issue of notes payable in Spanish

milled dollars.[86] The following year, on April 6, 1776, a committee

of seven was appointed "to examine and ascertain the value of several

[85] Hamilton MSS, I, pp. 1231, 1239, 1267, 1270, 1277
[86] A. Barton Hepburn, History of Coinage and Currency in the
United States, p. 12

- 69 -

species of gold and silver coins, current in these colonies, and the proportions they ought to bear to the Spanish milled dollar."[87] The committee rated the value of gold bullion at $17 and the value of silver bullion at $1 1/9 per Troy oz., thereby establishing a ratio of 15.3:1.[88]

In August, 1778, the Congress of the Confederation appointed another Committee with Robert Morris as chairman, to consider the state of money and finance in the United States. No action being taken, Morris was again instructed in January, 1782, to prepare a table of rates at which various coins should be received at the Treasury. The essence of Morris' recommendations, which plan, incidentally, was the work of Gouverneur Morris,[89] was: a silver standard, the quarter; coins consisting of a silver mark, quint, cent, a copper eight and five, based on a modified form of the decimal system, a coinage charge, and a ratio of $14\frac{1}{2}$:1 between gold and silver. Two thousand dollars was spent by Robert Morris in the attempt to establish the mint of North America.[90] Three or four dies were struck, but no real issue took place.

In 1783, Jefferson was asked to report on a coinage system. He, too, suggested the Spanish milled dollar as a standard since it was in general use, the decimal system with divisions of a $10 gold piece, silver $1.00, 50 cents, 20 cents, 10 cents, 5 cents,

87   Journal of Continental Congress - reprinted in International
     Monetary Conference Report, p. 419
88   MSS Reports, Committee on Finance, Ibid, p. 422
89   Neil Carothers, Fractional Money, p. 46. See also Spark's
     Life of Gouveneur Morris.
90   MSS Reports. Superintendant of Finance, I - reprinted in
     Report of International Monetary Conference, p. 425

and a copper penny, coinage of the standard at 11/12ths fine, a
bimetallic standard with a ratio of 15:1.[91]

These two reports resulted in the legislation of July
6, 1785, and August 8, 1786. The former adopted the Spanish milled
dollar as the standard and accepted the decimal system of coinage.
The latter made more detailed plans, fixing the fineness of gold
and silver coins at 11/12ths, providing coins of a silver dollar,
half dollar, doubledimes, dimes, and a copper cent, one-half cent
and a mill, adopting a ratio of 15.25:1 and favoring a coinage
charge.[92]

On July 6, 1787, a design for United States coins was
adopted.[93] "United States" was to be stamped in a circle and inside
this the inscription "We are one." On the other side was to be
the motto, "Mind your business," supposed to have been suggested by
Franklin.[94]

Hamilton had faithfully studied the legislation previously
cited, in particular that of July 6, 1785, and August 8, 1786. It
is evident from the references cited that he also examined the systems
of coinage and coins of European countries, especially England, France,
Spain and Portugal, "with whom we had trade." [95] Yet, in his Report,
Hamilton based his recommendations almost entirely on those previously
made and adopted by the Continental Congress. He suggested a bimetallic

91 Report of International Monetary Conference of 1878, pp. 437-443
92 Ibid, p. 445
93 J. B. McMaster, History of the U.S., I, p. 403
94 David Watson, History of American Coinage, p. 25. See also Benton's
   Abridgement of Debates on Devices of Coins, I, II
95 Lodge, IV, p.25

standard with a ratio of 15:1; the decimal system of coinage
with divisions of gold $10 and $1.00 pieces, a silver $1.00
and dime, and a copper penny and half-penny; no coinage charge
(with the exception of an individual's desiring immediate coinage);
a standard gold dollar of 24.75 grains and a standard silver dollar
(based on the old Spanish milled dollar) of 371.25 grains. Both
silver and gold coins were to be 11/12ths fine.[96]

Bimetallism had previously been advised by Jefferson.
Hamilton considered the question carefully, especially since no
other country at this time had a pure bimetallic standard. He
heartily favored it, since it would secure greater circulating
media for the country. (This reasoning, of course, is incorrect).
To use Hamilton's own words, a single standard could not be adopted
effectually "without destroying the office and character of one of
them (the metals) as money, abridging the quantity of circulating
medium and diminishing the utility of one as a metal."[97] If, however, a single standard were to be adopted he preferred gold because
of its greater stability, intrinsic superiority, rarity, and the
prejudices of mankind. But a single standard of gold was highly
improbable, since silver was the metal most in common use.[98]
Furthermore, Hamilton had the idea that general utility is best
promoted by gold for large, and silver for small payments.

96 Ibid.,p. 24
97 Ibid.,p. 15
98 Henry R. Linderman, Money and Legal Tender in the U.S., p. 14

Having decided on a bimetallic standard, Hamilton,
aware of its dangers, was most careful about setting the proper
ratio between the two metals. He cited the effect of an incorrect ratio, such as banishment of the undervalued metal,
diminution of the total quantity of specie which a country ought
to possess, greater and more frequent disturbances of the relation between units by greater and more frequent diversity between
the legal and market proportions of the metals.[99]

The selection of the ratio was difficult. Going back as
far as 1717, Hamilton quoted Sir Isaac Newton in a report to the
Treasury of Great Britain: "By the course of trade and exchange
between nation and nation in all Europe, fine gold is to fine silver as 14-4/5 or 15:1."[100] Realizing that this ratio could not
be accepted at a distance of seventy years for determining the
existing proportion, Hamilton looked elsewhere. From the references
previously cited, he found the proportion in the commercial market
of Holland in December, 1789, to be 1:14.88, in England approximately 1:15, in the United States 1:15. Since the mean proportion in
the commercial world market, 1:15, coincided with that in our own
market, Hamilton adopted the ratio. We must remember, this was also
the ratio which Jefferson had selected.

This occasion marks the first attempt in the world to

[99] Ibid, p. 17
[100] Ibid, p. 21

adopt by law a bimetallic standard, with all the requisite features of free and unlimited coinage of both metals, giving full legal tender to both.[101] It launched the United States upon a century of experiment as to the validity of the functioning of "Gresham's Law." In the opinion of Professor Laughlin "there probably never was a better example of a double standard, one more simple or one for whose successful trial, conditions could have been more favorable."[102] Furthermore, Hamilton's ratio was in accordance with the market ratio of 1792. No one at this time was aware that the production of silver was on the increase. As early as 1803, our bimetallic standard was disturbed because France adopted a ratio of $15\frac{1}{2}$:1.

On the question of a coinage charge, Hamilton, even after having examined the recommendations of Jefferson and Morris, was not in favor of it. Coinage in England was free. In Holland there was a duty of 1% on gold and $1\frac{1}{2}$% on silver, in France there was an 8 % duty.[103] Turgot, the late Minister of Finance in France, did not attribute any particular economic advantages to the duty on coinage. Hamilton, quoting Turgot, decided to abandon the idea of a coinage charge. He thought that the high rates of Morris' and Jefferson's reports might discourage coinage and "might influence prices in international relations, being in effect a reduction of

101 Hepburn, p. 24
102 J. Lawrence Laughlin, History of Bimettalism in U.S., p. 23
103 Lodge, IV, pp. 26-27

the standard of the coin as compared with bullion." Thus free coinage was suggested. To placate the coinage charge advocates, Hamilton recommended $\frac{1}{2}\%$ on gold and silver, if the depositor decided to receive his coins immediately.

The decimal system was adopted without any hesitation because of its convenience and simplicity. Gouverneur Morris, in the report on coinage submitted by Robert Morris, convinced the Congress of the Confederation of its superiority over every other system. Jefferson made it a salient proposal in his report the following year. On July 6, 1785, the decimal system of notation was adopted for the first time in any country.[104] However, neither Jefferson nor Gouverneur Morris seems to merit his biographer's claim of having introduced the decimal system into this country. Gouverneur Morris officially proposed it to Congress and convinced that body of its merits. The idea was first propounded by Stevin de Bruges in his pamphlet La Disme written in the 16th century.[105] Since then, there had been continued agitation for the displacement of the duodecimal (reckoning by twelves) and vigesimal (reckoning by twenties) systems of Europe, by the simple decimal system. It was not adopted by the European countries, mostly because of their traditional reluctance to make changes, as well as the difficulties of introducing a new system

[104] Hepburn, p. 52
[105] Carothers, p. 49

where an old one is well established. But, inasmuch as the
United States was creating a new financial system, this was the
time to incorporate all valid suggestions and innovations. Thus
the decimal system, for whose simplicity our European friends
envy us, was taken from theory and put into practice for the first
time.

A standard of 24.75 grains of gold and 371.25 grains of
pure silver was suggested. This was selected for two reasons:
in dealing with merchants in the country the gold dollar was
valued at 24.75 grains. Since the bimetallic ratio would be 15:1,
15 times 24.75 gave 371.25. Furthermore, the resolution of July 6,
1785 had adopted it. There was no question as to the use of alloy
because of the saving of expense in refining metals. All Europe
utilized it, and, to quote Hamilton, "it is a saving of trouble and
expense to follow European models." England, France, Spain, and
Portugal coined their gold standard at 11/12ths fine.[106] Jefferson
and Congress in the Act of August 8, 1786, had accepted this.
With these precedents, Hamilton did not hesitate to follow their
suggestions.

As to the number, kinds and denominations of coins,
Hamilton followed Jefferson's recommendations. The denominations
of coins, he contended, would have to be changed, for "mankind

[106] History of Coins and Coinage in the United States. By an old
Merchant, 1876 (1792-1876)

are much led by sounds and appearances."[107] A currency changing
its name will seem to have changed its nature. Consequently,
Jefferson's divisionsinto the eagle, dollar, dime and mill were
adopted; a gold $10, $1.00, a silver $1.00, 10 cents, a copper
penny, $\frac{1}{2}$ penny coins were proposed. The number of coins, Hamilton
thought, should be determined by convenience of circulation and
cheapness of coinage. He contended that numerous and small sub-
divisions assisted circulation; but on the other hand, a multiplica-
tion of the smaller increased expense.[108] Being of a practical
bent of mind, he advised beginning with a small number of coins
and then determining whether more would be needed.

The arrangement concerning foreign coins was to be as
follows. They were to circulate for one year, the privilege
extended for another year for the gold coins of Portugal, England
and France and still another year for the silver coins of these
countries. After three years, the circulation of foreign coins
would cease.[109]

Plans for the organization of the mint were included
in the Report, providing for a director, assay-master, a master
coiner, cashier and clerks.

The foregoing facts lead to the conclusion that there
was nothing creative about Hamilton's plan for mint and coinage.

---

[107] Lodge, III, 337
[108] Ibid, IV, 48
[109] The time for circulation of foreign gold and silver coins was
extended by the Actsof February 1, 1798, April 10, 1806, April 29, 1816
March 3, 1819. This was due to the fact that our own mint could not
furnish enough coins to take care of the country's needs. Hepburn, p. 26.
Foreign coins did not disappear from circulation until the late 1820's.

After having studied the European systems, he was all the more convinced of the merits of Morris' and Jefferson's recommendations. Consequently, his plan was more of the nature of selection than of creation.

Report on Manufactures:-

The Report on Manufactues, the most important and most quoted of Hamilton's works, has always been considered an Olympian accomplishment. The two editions of Hamilton's works by H.C. Lodge (1885 and 1904) and the still earlier edition of John C. Hamilton, give us the finished product. Nowhere has there been any indication of Hamilton's labor on the Report on Manufactures. The general impression is, that upon the request of Congress, Hamilton sat down and from his genius sprang the billiant classic. The Hamilton Manuscripts reveal that this was not so. Before making his final draft, Hamilton labored painstakingly over several. He practically wrote a volume in his attempt to prepare the Report on Manufactures.

The following works are cited in the Manuscripts:

Adam Smith's Wealth of Nations.
Hume's Balance of Trade.
The Commerce of Amsterdam, 6th Edition, 1744.[110]

No exact quotations are given except from Smith's Wealth

---

110 Hamilton MSS, III, 1775; XVII, 2295

of Nations. These will be treated later. The various drafts
mark no essential change in Hamilton's views on commerce and manufactures. They represent, rather, an addition or elimination of
facts and indicate the great labor required of the Secretary of
the Treasury to write the Report on Manufactures.

The Report was not Hamilton's first consideration of
the country's state of commerce. In 1781 and 1782, when the
commercial policies of the nation were as yet undetermined,
Hamilton wrote the Continentalist papers. These essays were an
attack upon the system of "laissez-faire", propounded by Adam
Smith. He decried the contention that "trade will regulate itself
and is not to be benefited by the encouragements or restrictions
of a government."[111] The Smithian system was indicted as "one of
those wild speculative paradoxes" which was contrary to the uniform
practice of nations. This marks the first challenge to Smith's
doctrine.

The essence of Hamilton's ideas at this period is
definitely Mercantilism. He considered commerce to have its fixed
principles, according to which it must be regulated. The leading
policy of a nation should be to preserve the balance of trade in
its favor. Not to be unsupported by theorists, Hamilton quoted
Hume:

[111] Lodge, I, 268

> The nature of the government, its spirit, maxims,
> or laws, in respect to trade are among those con-
> stant moral causes which influence its general
> results and when it has by accident taken a wrong
> direction, assist in bringing it back to its
> natural course. 112

This remark was followed by instances of the success of government

guidance in England, France, and Holland. In England, trade rose

under the auspices of Elizabeth and "its rapid progress there is

in a great measure to be ascribed to the fostering care of the

government in that and in succeeding reigns."[113] France, a little

later, was in the same prosperous condition due to the abilities

and indefatigable endeavors of "the great Colbert", who "laid

the foundations of French commerce and taught the way to his

successors to enlarge and improve it."[114] Holland likewise had

made the regulation of trade an essential object of the state.

Hamilton cited their commercial regulations as being more numerous

and rigid than any other country. "It is by a judicious and

unremitted vigilance of the government that they have been able to

extend their traffic to a degree so much beyond their natural and

comparative advantage."

There was also the question of revenue. Hamilton admitted

that imposts would be the best source. Here he stated definitely,

citing experience, that "moderate duties are more productive than

high ones," for with low duties the United States "can trade

112 Ibid, p. 270
113 Ibid, p. 270
114 Ibid, p. 278

abroad on better terms, its imports and exports will be larger, the duties will be regularly paid and arising out of a greater quantity of commodities will yield more in the aggregate than when they are so high as to operate either as a prohibition or as an inducement to evade them by illicit practices."[115] In two other instances in the Continentalist essays, Hamilton revealed his inclination towards moderate duties.

Ten years later, on December 5, 1791, Hamilton presented the Report on Manufactures to Congress. This essay is the best authority concerning the commercial development of the country at the close of the 18th century. It is the first detailed examination of the resources of the United States and of the means for their development. The first part of the Report is primarily devoted to a discussion of the necessity of encouraging the development of manufacturing industries in the United States. The second part is a summary of the state of production in the country and in particular an analysis of the industries which needed protection. Hamilton in making this broad survey of the field of manufactures, gathered the facts for his report by a most careful and searching method. A letter was sent to a citizen in every state and that citizen, by extensive correspondence, acquired from the surrounding towns and counties the facts desired by the Secre-

115 Ibid, p. 279

tary of the Treasury. The letters are of great interest, amusing
in a certain sense, when one reads with what enthusiasm and sincerity
such postscripts as that of John Mix from New Haven, Connecticut,
were written, "I would willingly Accept a Government Contract and
would furnish Buttons at a reasonable Rate and would put U.S.A.
on each Button."[116] Various producers even sent samples of their
manufactures. In the Hamilton Manuscripts there are twenty-one
pieces of black lace, very elaborately and intricately made.[117] They
are still intact. They are undoubtedly samples sent by a lace
manufacturer. Agents and representatives of the Treasury Department, collectors of customs and surveyors of posts all were engaged
in gathering information. During this period, Tench Coxe was
Hamilton's chief assistant in the preparation of the Report,
gathering much of the material contained therein. There is no
doubt that Hamilton exchanged ideas with Coxe, and was influenced
by his views favoring protection.[118] Furthermore, the letters
sent to Hamilton all indicated the difficulties with which American
industries were confronted and many appealed for protection.[119]

In order to understand the situation more concretely,
Hamilton interested himself in the establishment of a cotton
manufacturing plant at Paterson, New Jersey, erected by the
Society for Establishing Useful Manufactures. The prospectus

116 Arthur Cole, Industrial and Commercial Correspondence of
Alexander Hamilton, p. 52.
117 Hamilton MSS, XII, 1321
118 Harold Hutcheson, Life of Tench Coxe, pp. 99 and 100
     "There can be little doubt that Coxe played an important role in
the preparation of the famous Report on Manufactures." p. 99
     "The extent to which Hamilton made use of the ideas of Coxe in
drafting his Report is impossible to determine exactly upon the basis of
available material." p. 100
119 Cole, p. 52

written by Hamilton, strangely enough, gave an "ordered expression
to a group of ideas which reappeared three months later in a
famous state paper." [120] Herein Hamilton considered the establishment of manufactures in the United States to be "of highest importance to their prosperity" .... "Theory and experience conspire
to prove that a nation cannot possess much active wealth, but as
the result of extensive manufactures." Hamilton recommended New
Jersey as the seat of the new plant because of its relatively dense
population and abundant and cheap labor. Subscriptions for share's
to the company were to be made one half in funded 6% stock or 3%
stock (2 for 1) and the other half in 6% deferred stock.[121] Two
weeks before Hamilton submitted his report to Congress, the company
was incorporated by the state of New Jersey.

In the same year, 1791, an inquiry was made by a Congressional Committee into the state of trade. The results
revealed the restrictions which obstructed American trade. "Our
tobaccos are heavily dutied in England, Sweden, and France and
prohibited in Spain and Portugal", ... "our breadstuff is at most
times under prohibitory duties in England."[122] Apparently the
Tariff Act of 1789 was inadequate in its protection. Hamilton
thereupon studied the rates and pertinent facts regarding the
initiation of this protective tariff. Duties were partly ad

[120] Joseph S. Davis, Essays in the Earlier History of American
Corporations, I, 357
[121] Cole, p. 193
[122] American State Papers, Finance, I, pp. 300-324

valorem and partly specific, ranging from 5% - 10½%.[123] Linen and

cotton goods not mentioned in the tariff paid 5%. A deduction of

10% was allowed on goods imported in ships built or owned by

Americans. Congress was in session but two days when Madison had

introduced these tariff proposals.[124] Approval was almost unanimous.

Maclay, dissenting, asked "if we were not called by gratitude to

treat with discrimination those nations who had given us a helping

hand in distress."[125] The suggestion was immediately condemned.

"It was echoed from all parts of the House that nothing but

interest governed all nations."[126]

Such are the preliminaries to Hamilton's Report. He

was called upon by the House of Representatives for facts con-

cerning the manufactures of the country and "the measures of

promoting such as will tend to render the United States inde-

pendent of foreign nations for military and other essential

supplies."[127] Strictly fulfilling his orders, Hamilton laid out

his plans. His careful survey of manufactures, his own personal

experience, the recommendations of Congress, the circumstances

of the Tariff of 1789, and the requests of manufacturers con-

vinced him of the necessity of protection. In addition to this

and of great importance was the success of his financial program.

He needed sources of steady revenue for the newly launched

123 Comparative Tables of Present and Past Tariffs, Treasury Dept., p. 117
124 Francis A. Walker, Making of a Nation, p. 84
125 Maclay, p. 50
126 Ibid, p. 81
127 Lodge, IV, 70

fiscal measures. The protective tariff of 1789 had furnished
the government with considerable revenue and, as a matter of
fact, was practically the only source of Federal revenue.
Hence Hamilton's Report advised a tariff on the average 5%
higher than the Tariff of 1789.[128] Duties were to be increased
on "those articles which are the rivals of the domestic ones to
be encouraged,"[129] such as iron, cocoa, flax and hemp products,
liquors, etc. On the other hand, such raw materials as we could
not produce or lacked sufficient quantity of would be exempt
from duty, as tools, implements, silk, saltpeter and copper in
its three forms -- brass plates, pigs, and bars. A provision
was also made for importing duty-free raw material of a quality
superior to our own.[130]

To stimulate new enterprises, Hamilton advised a system
of premiums and bounties. Premiums or financial stipends were to
be given to reward a certain excellence or superiority in the
production of wool, silk, and fossil coal, which apparently were
inferior in quality to those of Europe. Hamilton cited this
method as having been very successful in England and Scotland.[131]
Bounties would be special stipends to encourage the manufacture
of a certain product. Here, Hamilton mentioned the $12\frac{1}{2}$% average
bounty of Great Britain on linens which "not only encourages their

[128] Ugo Rabbeno, American Commercial Policy, p. 34
[129] Ibid.
[130] Lodge, p. 154
[131] Ibid. p.153

manufacture, but increases their possibility of meeting competition
with other countries."

It is obvious from the above that Hamilton borrowed
considerably from Colbert. But it would be a mistake to assert,
as Professor Sumner does, that he was a confirmed mercantilist.
Hamilton actually belonged to no school nor approved of any system
per se. He was above all a nationalist, viewing the question of
protection from a political standpoint. National unity, security,
prosperity and economic and political independence were his objectives. He considered the tariff policy as a means to these
objectives. Colonial and English experience would have to be
followed to improve the commercial status of the United States.
There was no fast rule; modifications were to be made as needs
and circumstances changed. In 1790, the mercantilist policies
of England and France made a similar policy necessary. Hamilton
expressly mentioned "the embarrassments which have obstructed our
external trade -- the restrictive regulations which in foreign
markets, abridge the vent of the increasing surplus of agricultural products."[132] British laws further prevented the emigration
of mechanics and the export of machinery. Now that we were an
independent nation, it was necessary to make similar restrictions.
Thus Hamilton based his recommendations on expediency. The

[132] _Ibid_, p. 70

Mercantilist policies were not adopted because Hamilton was
convinced of their absolute validity in theory and practice, but
because after a careful consideration of other popular theories,
he found them poor instruments to attain his objectives.

The doctrine of Quesnay and the Physiocrats regarding
the unproductiveness of manufactures and the preference to be
given agriculture was repudiated. But, inasmuch as it governed
the economic thought of the Anti-Federalists, Hamilton exposed
its fallacies. Hamilton showed that agriculture had a "strong
preeminence" but not an "exclusive predilection" to every other
kind of industry.[133] There was "no material difference" between
the aggregate productiveness of agriculture and that of manufactures. One as well as the other would increase the revenue of
society. Briefly, he emphasized the interdependence of the two
industries and the necessity of developing them jointly for the
material well-being of the nation. As to the unproductiveness of
manufactures, he maintained, "There is no proof of this contention and the arguments proving it are rather subtle and para-
doxical, than solid or convincing."[134] He argued for the productiveness of manufactures, since it would allow a larger
application of the principle of division of labor, extend the use
of machinery, give additional employment, stimulate emigration

[133] Ibid, p. 74
[134] Ibid, p. 87

from foreign countries, furnish greater scope for diversity of
talents of men, afford more ample fields for enterprise and
create a steady and increased demand for the products of agriculture. With the conclusion that "most general theories,
however, admit of numerous exceptions and there are few, if any
of the political kind, which do not blend as considerable a
portion of the error of the truths they inculcate,"[135] Hamilton
rejected Physiocracy.

He next analyzed the free trade and "let alone"
theories of Adam Smith. He challenged the contention "that
if industry is left to itself it will naturally find its way
to the most useful and profitable employment, and that manufactures without government aid will grow up as soon and as
fast as necessary to the interests of the state and people."
For, as Hamilton contended, "the simplest improvements are
adopted with reluctance and by slow gradations." There is the
factor of "strong influence of habit and the spirit of imitation,
the fear of want of success in untried enterprises, the intrinsic
difficulties incident to first essays towards a competition with
those who have previously attained perfection in the business"
and "the bounties, premiums, and other artificial encouragements
with which foreign nations second the exertions of their own

[135] _Ibid_, p. 73

citizens in the branches in which they are to be rivaled"
which would invalidate Smith's theory in the United States in
her early stage of development. Finally, there was sufficient
evidence in Hamilton's correspondence with American manufacturers
that industry did not want to be "left to itself".[136]

Although Hamilton dissented from Smith's principles
of free trade, he did not reject them wholly. He admitted the
advantages of free trade provided it be in universal use. In
other words, free trade, theoretically, and as a final conclusion, was desirable.[137] But the United States was a new country,
with very small manufactures and a very large market. To face a
world whose commercial policy was one of restriction and
taxation with a policy of free trade would mean destruction. It
was necessary to encourage manufactures, to increase our industrial enterprises and to meet discrimination with discrimination in order to maintain our independence and build a powerful
nation. Thus, owing to economic circumstances in the United
States, protection was necessary. England in its stage of
economic development could afford free trade; the United States
could not. To quote Rabbeno, "Hamilton is a protectionist who
admits unconditionally the advantages of free trade when it is
universally applied and who advocates reciprocity of treatment

136 Ibid, p. 104
137 Ibid, p. 38

between nations rather than protection as a principle."[138] He
was a protectionist who severely criticized high protective
duties and who suggested a relatively moderate scheme for
protection.

Cossa has aptly said, "Economic writers are almost
always influenced, though·in varying degrees, by the specific
conditions, ideas, and institutions of their country and the
period to which they belong."[139] So it is with Hamilton. He
represented Smith's system of free trade as possible in practice
if adopted by all nations simultaneously. As he observed,
"Reasons of expediency justify departure from this wise and
liberal policy, reasons peculiar in their nature and temporary
in their influence dictate this action to the country by the
imperious force of a very peculiar situation." Without capital
at home and without credit abroad, the soundest policy was to
arouse, strengthen and increase the manufacture of this
country by whatever means possible. The following will give an
idea as to the practical bent of Hamilton's thoughts. "The
expediency of encouraging domestic manufactures rests not upon
reasoning but on facts and upon circumstances which create an
exception to the general rule."[140] In 1791 he wrote to Jefferson,
"My commercial system turns very much on giving free course to

138 Rabbeno, p. 309
139 Luigi Cossa, Introduction to the Study of Political Economy, p. 113
140 Lodge, IV, 109

trade and cultivating good humor with all the world."[141] Three
years later he prepared a project for the treaty of reciprocity
with England, later to be used by Jay, wherein he agreed to
stipulations limiting the tax on all leading American manufactured
articles to 10%.[142]

In answer to Jefferson's message to Congress in 1801,
referring to the possible increase of duties on imports, Hamilton
remarked,

> It is in a degree questionable whether it may
> not be found necessary to reduce the rates.
> That they are now high when compared with the
> commercial capital of the country is not to be
> denied and whether they may not be found too
> high for a beneficial course of trade is yet
> to be decided by experiment. [143]

Hamilton fully acknowledged the advantages that would
accrue from all nations adopting a system of perfect liberty and
free trade,

> In such a state of things, each country would
> have full benefit of its peculiar advantages
> to compensate for its deficiences or dis-
> advantages. If one nation were in a condition
> to supply the manufactured articles on better
> terms than another, that other might find
> abundant indemnification in its superior capacity
> to furnish the produce of the soil. And a free
> exchange mutually beneficial, of commodities
> which each was able to supply on the best terms
> might be carried on between them, supporting in
> full vigor the industry of each .... But the
> system which has been mentioned is far from
> characterizing the general policies of nations.[144]

Thus, after an exhaustive search for a system of trade, Hamilton

---

141 William G. Sumner, Lectures on the History of Protection in the
United States, p. 180
142 Lodge, p. 313
143 Ibid, VIII, 255
144 Ibid, IV, 101

chose protection. He defended his choice with a quotation from
David Hume's <u>Balance of Trade</u> that "government interference is
not useless or hurtful."

It was Hamilton's rationalization of his convictions
that led Professor Sumner to accuse him of being "full of confusion
and contradiction" in his famous Report.[145] But, in the author's
opinion, Hamilton's reasoning is sound and conclusive. It was
necessary to analyze the advantages and disadvantages of the
leading commercial theories, and then select the one which would
satisfy the economic demands of the country.

The Report on Manufactures is often considered the
initial step in the history of American protectionism. It has
been used and abused as the foundation and authority upon which
afterwards was laid every argument for an increase of the protective tariff. Hamilton has not been given the credit due him
for his impartial and scientific reasoning. His tariff proposals were moderate with two objectives: revenue and protection.
They were definitely low in contrast to the rates a century
later. In 1792, following Hamilton's report, duties were increased by only $2\frac{1}{2}\%$ above those of 1790, and 5% above those of
1789. In twenty years following, however, customs duties
were nearly trebled.

[145] Sumner, p. 179

The protectionist's logic is somewhat faulty. Thompson
ascribes the unusual progress in the foreign trade of the United
States after 1791 to the enactment of protective tariffs.[146] In
reality the true stimuli to the commercial activity of the early
1790's were the political events of Europe. Hence, this is no .
basis on which to excuse the higher protective tariffs following
the War of 1812.

On this question of the origin of American protection,
there are two schools of thought, Bishop, Bolles, Thompson, and
Mason think that the Act of 1789 initiated the system of protection.
Ely, Taussig and Henry C. Adams contend otherwise. In the opinion
of the latter authorities, the early tariffs were financial and
political measures, and the American system of protections was not
initiated until after the War of 1812.[147] Adams asserts that
Hamilton was seeking revenue to procure income and reestablish
public credit and not "to establish the manufacture of beer bottles."[148]
Hamilton desired to strengthen the union of the states and stimulate
commercial activities between them.[149] The conclusions of Smith
and Seligman are that "a careful review of the debates in Congress,
and the discussions by the public and the provisions of the act
itself show clearly that the paramount consideration was that of
revenue. The chief need of the times was adequate provision for

146 Thompson, History of the United States, pp. 84 and 85
147 Henry C. Adams, Taxation in the United States, 1884, pp. 32-37
148 Ibid, p. 62
149 Richard T. Ely, Problems of Today, p. 42

Government expenses; and the manufacturing interests were so
utterly insignificant that the main stress was laid on the revenue
features......The same is practically true of all the tariff Acts
until the close of the War of 1812 with England."[150]

The writer's opinion is to the contrary. Hamilton did
not want a tariff primarily for revenue with incidental protection.
Furthermore, manufacturing interests were not insignificant. This
statement cannot be made if one has read Hamilton's correspondence
with the manufacturing interests and the several drafts he made in
preparation of his report. The necessity of moderate protection
to establish our manufactures is Hamilton's main concern. The desire for revenue is incidental and is scarcely mentioned in comparison with the other objective. All of Hamilton's recommendations were made with the intent of building a strong central government. To give a moderate protective tariff to the manufacturing
interests (which they greatly desired) would not only win their
support, but would encourage their activities, which would in time
develop the country's economy.

It is in this Report on Manufactures that Hamilton quotes
Smith in so many instances. In three distinct passages Smith's
textual words are quoted at length: first, in a criticism of the
Physiocratic doctrine; second, in a demonstration of the advantages

---

[150] Smith and Seligman, Commercial Policies of U.S., 1892. Lupzig

of the division of labor; third, in discussion of the advantages
of the development of the means of transportation. His criticism
of the Physiocrats corresponds precisely with the third and fourth
observations made by Smith. The idea is merely a recapitulation
of the words of the original author. From Smith he borrowed the
idea of the division of labor, the opinion that it finds better
application in manufactures than in agriculture, and an enumeration
and illustration of the advantages of the technical division of
labor. The three advantages he puts forth are Smith's: 1.) Skill
acquired by an artisan always occupied in the same task; 2.) The
saving of time expended in passing from one operation to another;
3.) The larger use of machinery, invention being rendered easier
by division of labor. Edward G. Bourne has paralleled at least
twenty passages from Hamilton's Report on Manufactures with Adam
Smith's Wealth of Nations.[151] This is sufficient evidence to
nullify Sumner's contention that "Hamilton had not read Adam Smith."
Further proof is in the fact that in two instances in the Manuscripts,
references are given to Smith's Wealth of Nations. They are in
Hamilton's handwriting and the source is marked, the Wealth of
Nations, giving volume, book, chapter and page. Bourne in his study
of Adam Smith and Alexander Hamilton apparently used Lodge's edition
of Hamilton's works. Since Lodge did not publish the worksheet, but

---

151 Edward Bourne, Alexander Hamilton and Adam Smith, Quarterly
Journal of Economics, 1893, VIII, pp. 328-344

only the final report, Bourne concluded that Hamilton had not
made any references to Smith. Naturally then, he did not understand
why Hamilton failed to give credit to his source. He concluded it
was for "political expediency." To have quoted an English economist
at this time would have nullified the merits of a worthwhile suggestion.

The references to Smith's Wealth of Nations in the
Hamilton Manuscripts are the following: Volume I, Book 2, Chapter 2,
pages 441-444 and Volume I, page 219. In the former, Smith discusses
the advantages of banks.[152] The quotation being too lengthy,
Hamilton only refers to it to prove his contention that "it is agreed
among sound theorists that banks more than compensate for the loss of
specie in other ways." In the latter reference, Hamilton quotes
directly the passage, "Good roads, canals ..... since that time.", to
show that improvements in the country have important relations to
manufactures.[153]

It is necessary to say a few final words in estimation
of Hamilton and his work. Perhaps his greatest work has been
the mould cast for the country's development, and the impression
made on the political thought of the country. Until Hamilton
set down and forced through his policies, there was no successful

[152] Hamilton MSS, XIII, p. 1775
[153] Ibid, XVII, p. 2295

attempt at organization of the economic machine. The experience
of England was a valuable guide and was used to the utmost.

 With the passing of more than a century, there is little
that is obsolete in Hamilton's system. The institutions established
have been operative throughout our history and are still efficient
in giving shape and direction to our national life. The basic services of the treasury and the assembly of revenues are the same today as when Hamilton left them. Financial historians have remarked
on Hamilton's elastic system, on its expansion and adaptability
to changed conditions. Hamilton constructed the original treasury
machine so well that it has never been materially altered. Gallatin
after microscopic quest for taint reported "that in no respect could
the department be improved." In the administrations of Hamilton's
political foes, Jefferson, Madison and Monroe, the treasury operated
on the same principles and under the same agencies. In 1920 in a
letter to Secretary Mellon, Mr. Warshow, one of Hamilton's biographers,
made inquiry as to whether the organization of the Treasury as originally conceived by Hamilton was still in effect. Mr. Mellon replied
that 'Hamilton's organization is substantially continued, the operations today being conducted on the same structural plan as utilized
by the first Secretary of the Treasury."[154]

 We must admit that Hamilton was a man of pre-eminent ability.
His work was congenial and familiar to him. The knowledge of vast

[154] Warshow, p. 116

difficulties, instead of being a handicap, was a stimulus to
the arduous undertaking. Professor Beard in his <u>Economic Inter-</u>
<u>pretation of the Constitution</u> states "that the success of the
national government could not have been secured under any other
policy than that pursued by Hamilton."[155]

It is this work which evoked the eulogy from Webster,
"He smote the rock of national resources and abundant streams of
revenue gushed forth, he touched the dead corpse of public credit
and it sprang to its feet."[156]

[155] Charles A. Beard, <u>Economic Interpretation of the Constitution</u>
<u>of the United States, 1913</u>, p. 33 (footnote)
[156] Webster's speech on Hamilton, March 10, 1831

CHAPTER III

A VINDICATION OF HAMILTON

In a consideration of Hamilton's fiscal policies, it
is fitting that an attempt be made to vindicate him of the charges
and attacks that have been made against him. During the entire
period of his incumbency as Secretary of the Treasury, Hamilton
was charged with speculation, divulging important information to
his friends, misappropriation of funds, and with attempting to
burden the country with an excise, which after several years of
experiment, had proved a poor source of revenue. He was also
accused of considering the debt a national blessing, with intentions of making it perpetual. It will be well to examine these
indictments more carefully and to draw some conclusions.

As early as 1793 Hamilton was charged with making the
public money "subservient to loans, discounts and accommodations"
for himself and for his friends.[1] A House Committee investigated
these accusations thoroughly. Affidavits from employees and
various officials of the Bank of the United States were obtained.
The Treasury and Bank records were carefully examined, but the
results were favorable and Hamilton was exonerated.

The same year, Representative Giles placed his famous
charges against Hamilton. Giles, whose political philosophy was

[1] H.C. Lodge, Works of Alexander Hamilton, VI, 456

so opposed to Hamilton's, was always suspicious of Hamilton's
financial measures. He had not favored the sinking fund, the
funding system or the Bank. Now with Hamilton's policies well
in effect, he objected to their secrecy. It is true that Hamilton
had little patience with Congress, and especially with men like
Giles. Consequently, Congress was informed of the barest essentials. When Hamilton had written his First Report on the
Public Credit, Congress had refused him permission to deliver and
explain his Report in person. They preferred a written advisory
message. Thereafter, Hamilton saw little reason to antagonize
that body by disquisitions. All of his financial measures were
launched with the approval of Congress. But, impatient of delay,
Hamilton consulted himself as to details. Giles, resenting this
bold individualism, ascribed to Hamilton the following actions:

1) Failure to give Congress information of moneys drawn by him
   from Europe into the United States,[2]
2) Failure to remain within his authority in making loans,
3) Application of a certain portion of the borrowed principal
   to the payment of interest falling due upon the principal.
   This was not authorized by law.
4) Making provisions without appropriation by law.
5) Failure to consult public interest in negotiating a loan with

[2] Hamilton MSS, XVIII, 2515

the Bank of the United States and drawing therefrom $400,000.

6) Lack of decorum to the House in undertaking to judge its motives.

Three of the charges were rejected immediately. The others were given to a Committee of the House where after considerable debate they, too, were dropped.

On December 1, 1794, two months previous to his resignation, Hamilton sent a notice to the House of his intentions to return to his private law practice. He did this to give them an opportunity to "institute any further proceedings which may be contemplated", as to an inquiry into the state of his department. No further action on the part of Congress was ever taken.

In 1796, however, Gallatin, writing his Sketch of the Finances of the United States, accused Hamilton of being responsible for a poor accounting system, with no single department as a central accounting agency. Hamilton denied this charge, contending that all the moneys which had left the Treasury were accounted for by a single department. The other charge concerned a diversion of funds from one purpose to another. Hamilton, in admitting the truth of this statement, defended himself on the basis that it was absolutely necessary for efficiency. He contended that appropriations of specific funds for specific purposes could never be practicable, and gave the

following example: If the bad roads damage our wagons to such an
extent as to exhaust the specific appropriation for repairs, and,
on the other hand, if the consumption of forage is less than
expected, should not the surplus from the latter be used for
repair of the wagons? The question was closed until Gallatin
became Secretary of the Treasury, when a bill passed forbidding
general appropriations and making only specific appropriations
legal. The latter has proved its value. Although Hamilton's
method was superior from the standpoint of efficiency, Gallatin's
was safer.

Another public attack followed Hamilton's resignation.
In 1797, Callender, the notorious pamphleteer, published a series
of papers involving Hamilton, Duer, and Reynolds, which from
their contents gave the impression that Hamilton had speculated
with government funds. The story is that in 1792 a certain
Clingman, in jail with Reynolds because of a crooked transaction
with the government, communicated with Speaker Muhlenburg.
Clingman claimed that Reynolds "had in his possession papers
which would show that he and Hamilton had speculated together."
Muhlenburg, with Monroe and Venable, had this substantiated by
both Reynolds and his wife. Immediately they visited Hamilton
and demanded an explanation from him. The latter denied ever

having made any improper use of government funds and further denied having had any relations with Reynolds except through Mrs. Reynolds. This explanation was accepted and the question was dropped. It was agreed that the letters in the case were never to be published. Subsequently, Monroe was appointed Minister to Paris. In 1796, Washington, being dissatisfied with Monroe's services, recalled him. Monroe was infuriated and blamed Hamilton. The next episode was the publication of the papers. The matter was a sensation and a rather strong indictment of Hamilton's character and activities as keeper of the public purse. Rather than allow his public integrity to be sullied, Hamilton submitted himself to the worst possible personal humiliation. He replied in the famous Reynolds pamphlet. Therein he denied all charges against him as to the use of government funds in relations with Reynolds and gave in detail his personal relations with Mrs. Reynolds. (See Lodge, VII, the Reynolds Pamphlet).

The charge of speculating for his personal interest and that of his friends was perhaps the most popular one against Hamilton. The investigations which were made disclosed nothing incriminating against him. A study of his manuscripts proves that Hamilton himself never profited from any stock transactions. As a matter of fact, he held only a small amount of public stock.

In a letter to William Seton, June 26, 1792, he wrote, "All my
property in the funds is about $800 in 3%'s. These at a certain
period I should have sold had I not been unwilling to give
occasion to cavil."[3] At no time in his life was Hamilton considered a wealthy man. Upon his death, his debts far exceeded
his holdings, and a collection was taken up for his widow.

There seems to be some evidence against Hamilton as to
his speculation for his family's interest. In his Reminiscences
Hamilton's son said that Hamilton had requested his father-in-law,
General Schuyler, to keep his son from speculating in public
securities "lest it be inferred that their speculations were made
upon information furnished by Hamilton or were made in part on
Hamilton's account."[4] Schuyler, however, did not think that this
request pertained to him. An examination of the loan books of
the Treasury Department reveals that he was a large dealer in
stock in New York. For March, there was $23,189.21 to his
credit; for October, $15,594.61; for November, $20,689.21.

Hamilton's brother-in-law, John Church, also dealt
heavily in public securities during Hamilton's administration.
Church is credited with holdings of $28,187.91. The records show
that Hamilton bought and sold for Church through Thomas Willing
in Philadelphia, and William Seton in New York, the government's

---

[3] MSS, Treasury Department, Ledger E, Treasury 3%'s, XLIV, 434
[4] J.A. Hamilton, Reminiscences, p. 18

agents. A letter from Seton, dated February 24, 1790, reads in part, "I observe what you say respecting the sale of what remains of Mr. Church's shares and shall do whatever be in my power to dispose of them, whenever I receive the certificates and your orders to make the sale."[5] Several years later, March 21, 1793, Seton in writing to Hamilton complained that he could not make an investment for Church because of the present price of bank stock.[6] A few days later he informed Hamilton of the possibility of purchasing stocks within a day or so for Mr. Church "under your limits", and added, "I therefore feel loath to enter into the market without further orders from you."[7]

A communication from William Henderson, dated August 24, 1792, shows that Hamilton had bought 45,000 acres of land, apparently for Schuyler, Church and himself. Another land holding of Hamilton's consisted of five shares of Western land in the Ohio Company, proprietors of land on the Muskingum River.[8] A word may be said in Hamilton's behalf when he was called upon to decide the validity of the Company's claims to several thousand acres. He felt the delicacy of the situation and wrote to Washington, stating his interest in the lands and suggesting that the matter be referred to the accounting officers of the Treasury, with the Attorney-General giving the final opinion.[9]

5 Correspondence of Thomas Willing and Alexander Hamilton, XXIII, p. 1
6 Hamilton MSS, XX, 180
7 Ibid, p. 182
8 A.M. Dyer, Ownership of the Ohio Lands, p. 69
9 Washington MSS, Folio 291

It is obvious from the above that if Hamilton himself
did not speculate, he at least bought and sold stock for his
relatives.

There is still the question of divulging information to
his friends. When asked by Henry Lee about the possible rise of
securities in 1789, Hamilton answered,

> I am sure you are sincere when you say that you
> would not subject me to an impropriety, nor
> do I know that there would be any in answering
> your queries; but you remember the saying with
> regard to Caesar's wife. I think the spirit
> of it applicable to every man concerned in the
> administration of the finances of the country.
> With respect to the conduct of such men suspi-
> cion is ever eagle-eyed and the most innocent
> things may be misinterpreted. 10

After careful research, this remark summarizes Hamilton's conduct
in dealing with his friends.

We must remember, however, that it would have been
difficult for Hamilton to reorganize the finances of the country
without conferring with the leading financiers of the time. His
policy was to supervise the market and to keep it within bounds.
He kept in constant touch with them to prevent any extreme in
price. At times his advice and warnings went unheeded, as in
Duer's case.

On August 13, 1791 Rufus King in a letter cautioned
Hamilton against giving out statements which might affect prices,

10 J.A. Hamilton, p. 18

and informed him that his opinions had been quoted in efforts to
depress the stocks -- the opinion being "that the stocks are all
too high -- and prices below the present market as the Value
sanctioned by your authority."[11] King also spoke of Duer being
injured in the attempt to raise prices, but added that "so far
as I can learn, his conduct has been as correct as any buyer's
or seller's could be."

Two days later, Hamilton answered King, explaining
that he had given out his opinion on prices to counteract an
undue rise in script on the market. He concluded by giving
King the prices of the day, adding, "I will give you my standard
that you may be able if necessary to contradict insinuations of
an estimation on my part short of that standard for the purpose
of depressing the funds."[12]

Two other letters were written this same day by
Hamilton, one to Seton and the other to Duer. He informed Seton
that he was sending him $150,000, "to keep the stock from falling
too low."[13] On the other hand, he warned Duer against pushing
prices too high. He added,

> I will honestly own I had serious fears for you --
> for your purse and for your reputation; and with
> an anxiety for both, I wrote you in earnest terms.
> You are sanguine, my friend. You ought to be
> aware of it yourself and to be on your guard

[11] Hamilton MSS, XII, 1566
[12] Ibid, p. 1566
[13] Ibid, p. 1567

against the propensity. I do not widely differ
from you as to the real value of bank script.
I should rather call it within 90, to be within
bounds, with hopes of better things, and I
sincerely wish you may be able to support it
at what you mention. [14]

The only other reference to Duer is after his failure.
In a letter to Seton, October 10, 1791, Hamilton asks, "Does
Duer's failure affect the solidity of the government?"

The conclusion to be drawn from these few excerpts
is that information had to be given to the agents in charge of
buying and selling stock for the government. Not satisfied with
an injunction to stop at a fair profit, many of the speculators
bought heavily and lost heavily, but we can arrive at no indictment of Hamilton himself because of this.

Before closing the issue, it is only fair to consider
Hamilton's attitude toward the accusations of speculation made
against him. "Merely because I retained an opinion once common
to me, that the public debt ought to be provided for on the basis
of the contract upon which it was created, I have been wickedly
accused with wantonly increasing the public burthen many millions
in order to promote a stock-jobbing interest for myself and my friends."[15]
It is apparent from this remark that Hamilton's personal finances
were governed by principle and not by profit. His manuscripts show

14 Ibid, p. 1568. Also, Lodge, VIII, 234
15 Lodge, VI, 453

that he thought there was a great deal of exaggeration concerning speculation.[16] With respect to the certificates of the State Debts, he contended that speculation began only after the plan for assumption was given to the House in the First Report on the Public Credit. "The resources of individuals in this country are too limited to have admitted of much progress in purchases before the knowledge of that plan was diffused throughout the country. After that, purchasers and sellers were upon equal ground." Hamilton attributed the opposition in the South to Madison. The Southerners, entertaining so high an opinion of him, took it for granted that the opposition would be successful. The certificate holders were eager to part with them at current prices, calculating that the purchasers would suffer a loss from the securities' future fall. Furthermore, a great part of the debt which was purchased by the Northerners, was at a very high price.[17] In many instances, the price was above the true value. At one point speculation caused prices to rise 25% above par and upwards. Hamilton thought that the Southerners on the whole did not part with their property for nothing. "They parted with it voluntarily -- in most cases, upon fair terms, without surprise or deception, in many cases for more than its true value." He added that this was not conjectural but was "founded on information from intelligent

[16] Hamilton MSS, XVII, 2307
[17] Ibid, p. 2308

Southern Characters -- and may be obtained by inquiry."

Perhaps one of the most often repeated statements concerning Hamilton's debt policy is the fact that he thought a
national debt was a national blessing. This charge is unfounded.
A careful reading of the Reports and the Hamilton Manuscripts
reveals again and again his advice that "the creation of Debt
should always be accompanied by a provision for its extinction."

In the second letter to Morris, written April 30, 1780,
Hamilton said, "A national debt, if it is not excessive, will
be to us a national blessing. It will be a powerful cement of
our Union."[18] Hamilton never admitted nor did he deny this
statement. Thereafter, he took every precaution to choose his
words carefully and to assert on every occasion his desire for
payment of the debt.

In the First Report on the Public Credit, Hamilton
states that the "funding of the existing debt would render it a
national blessing." He expands this idea as follows:

> Persuaded as the Secretary is that a proper
> funding of the present debt will render it
> a national blessing, yet he is so far from
> acceding to the position in the latitude
> of which it is sometimes laid down, that
> "Public Debts are Public Benefits", a posi-
> tion inviting to prodigality and liable to
> dangerous abuse, that he ardently wishes to
> see it incorporated as a fundamental maxim

[18] Lodge, III, 42

in the system of public credit of the United
States, that the creation of debt should
always be accompanied with the means of
extinguishment. This he regards as the true
secret for rendering public credit immortal.[19]

He urged Congress,

To endeavor to establish it as a rule of the
administration that the creation of a debt
should always be accompanied with a provision
for its extinguishment and to apply the rule
as far as it could be applicable to a new
provision for an old debt by incorporating
with it a fund for sinking the debt. [20]

Hamilton was equally insistent against incurring new

debts. He gave his opinion in the Report on Manufactures,

Neither will it follow that an accumulation
of debt is desirable, because a certain degree
of it operates as capital .... The debt, too,
may be swelled to such a size that the greatest
part of it may cease to be useful as a capital,
serving only to pamper the dissipation of
idle and dissolute individuals; as that the
sums required to pay the interest upon it may
become oppressive and beyond the means which
a Government can employ consistently with its
tranquility to raise them; as that the resources of taxation to face the debt, may
have been strained too far to admit of ex-
tensions adequate to exigencies which regard
the public safety; .... and as the vicissi-
tudes of nations beget a perpetual tendency
to the accumulation of debt, there ought to be
in every government a perpetual, anxious and
unceasing effort to reduce that which at any
time exists, as fast as shall be practicable,
consistently with integrity and good faith. [21]

19 Ibid, p. 387
20 Ibid, VIII, 475
21 Hamilton MSS, XIV, 43

Even in so obscure a report as that relative to
additional supplies for carrying on the Indian War (March 16,
1792), Hamilton did not fail to repeat his advice,

> Nothing can more interest the national credit
> and prosperity than a constant and systematic
> attention to husband all the means previously
> possessed for extinguishing the present debt,
> and to avoid as much as possible, the incur-
> ring of any new debt. 22

Before resigning as Secretary of the Treasury, Hamilton submitted his last Report on the Public Credit. Final
effort was made "to promote that invaluable end" (that creation
of debt should always be accompanied with provisions for its
extinguishment). His advice was

> To avoid the ills of an excessive employ-
> ment of it (public credit) by true economy
> and system in the public expenditures; ....
> and by using sincere, efficient and per-
> servering endeavors to diminish present
> debts, prevent the accumulation of new, and
> secure the discharge within a reasonable
> period, of such as it may be at any time
> matter of necessity to contract. 23

The foregoing statements necessarily indicate the absurdity of
the charge that Hamilton was in favor of increasing the national
debt merely for the sake of doing so, on the ground that it was
a blessing per se.

The opinions concerning Hamilton's attitude toward the

22 Ibid, p. 44
23 Lodge, III, 300

excise have been so distorted that it is advisable to present
the issue in full.

On October 12, 1789, Hamilton wrote Madison for suggestions as to revenue. Madison, five weeks later (November 19)
replied,

> The question is very much what further taxes
> will be least unpopular ..... The supplemental
> funds which at present occur to me as on the
> whole most eligible, are from an excise on
> home distilleries. If the tax can be regulated
> by the size of the still it will shun every
> objection that renders excises unpopular or
> vexatious. Such an experiment was made in
> Scotland and as a Scotch tax I have not under-
> stood that the mode was disapproved. 24

This suggestion was immediately adopted by Hamilton.
In considering additional sources of revenue Hamilton proposed
the excise. Included in the First Report on Public Credit was
a schedule of duties and approximate calculations of their
revenue.

```
4,000,000 gals. distilled spirits
      imported from foreign countries at 8¢ gal. ---- $320,000
3,500,000 gals. distilled spirits
      produced in United States from foreign
      materials at 11¢ gal. -------------------------- $385,000
3,000,000 gals. distilled spirits
      produced in United States from domestic
      materials at 9¢ a gal. ------------------------- $270,000

Total --------------------------------------------- $975,000
Deduction from expenses of collection at 10% ------- 97,500

Net Profit ---------------------------------------- $877,500 25
```

24 Diplomatic Correspondence, VII, 321
25 American State Papers, Finance, I

But Congress was reluctant to make use of this tax.
They realized the disturbance it would cause in Pennsylvania,
Massachusetts and Connecticut. All these states had had an
excise tax for years, Pennsylvania from 1756,[26]-- but either had
never been able to collect it, or had never collected enough to
justify the law as a source of revenue. Today, we wonder how
there could have been any objection to a liquor tax. The colonists,
frontiersmen especially, apparently considered liquor a staple of
their diet. When the importation of rum was prevented by war,
they began to distill their own whiskey. Soon they realized that
were they to sell their product, a profit might be realized. The
transportation of corn to the market was difficult and expensive
and in the long run yielded them nothing. Consequently, they
resorted to a more profitable enterprise -- the distillation of
spirits.

Although Hamilton's proposal of the excise in his First
Report was not adopted, still Congress appealed to him again a
year later for additional sources of revenue. Hamilton was at a
loss to suggest any new tax and repeated his former proposal: a
further duty on foreign liquors, and a duty on liquors distilled
in the United States from foreign materials and from domestic
materials. The same schedule and calculations included in the

[26] Pennsylvania Archives

First Report were submitted. This time the promise of a revenue
of $877,500 appealed to Congress. A provision was made that if
the tax yielded any excess revenue, $50,000 of it was to be
pledged to the sinking fund. Since the duties on the great mass
of imported articles had reached a point "which it would not be
expedient to exceed", Congress adopted Hamilton's recommendations.
The Secretary of the Treasury feared the opposition that the
measure would encounter. Consequently, he placed many restrictions
on the collecting agents. Officers were to have no jurisdiction
to visit or search indiscriminately the houses and stores of
producers. The producers were to mark their stills as places
of distillation. Only then would they be approached.

For three years an attempt was made to put the act
into effect. Because of intense objection, within a year the
excise duty was reduced 15%.[27] The next step was to appease the
distillers by placing a duty on the monthly capacity of the still
rather than on the amount distilled. Options were granted to
producers of substituting a license tax on the monthly capacity
of the still. Producers improved their stills, thus increasing
the output. Consequently the tax fell to 3¢ a gallon, and later
to 3/5ths of a cent.[28] But still there was great opposition
to the law. In the four counties of Western Pennsylvania outrages

[27] American State Papers, Finance, I, 149
[28] D.R. Dewey, Financial History of the United States, p. 106

were perpetrated against those citizens who tried to abide by the
law. Distilleries which complied with the tax were burned; the
collecting officers were attacked; inspectors were tarred and
feathered. On September 6, 1793, the incensed distillers of
western Pennsylvania subjected the Collector of Revenue to such
extreme physical violence as to evoke the disgust of even the
officials of Pennsylvania.[29] Hamilton realized that only force
would have effect. With a militia of approximately 12,000 from
Maryland, Virginia, New Jersey and Pennsylvania, he and
Washington went to Pennsylvania to quell the insurrection (1794).

In an appeal to the public under the pseudonym Tully,
Hamilton listed the concessions that had been bootlessly made:
a lowering of the duties, a revision of the act in three successive congressional sessions, accommodations, considerations,
explanations and forebearances -- all for the convenience of the
taxed. Even an allowance of 2% for leakage and wastage in the
shipping of spirits from one state to another was made.[30] Hamilton
contended that liquor manufacture had attained its maturity, and
hence that the beverage was as fit an article of taxation as any
other. Furthermore, the duty in itself was no injury, since it
could be passed on to the consumer. As a matter of fact, the
excise had affected the price of whiskey. Previous to its passage,

[29] Lodge, III, 362
[30] Ibid, VI, 487

the price of liquor was 38¢, in 1794 it had risen to 56¢. Other
causes might have contributed in some degree to this rise, but
it is evidently to be ascribed chiefly to the duty. Exemptions
had been granted to stills of a capacity less than fifty gallons.
Almost no spirits could be purchased abroad except in a quantity
of fifty gallons or more. The tax on foreign liquors was increased
to such an extent that a consumer of foreign spirits had to pay ·
nearly three times the price of domestic ones.[31] It was contended
that the tax was especially distressing to the four western
counties of Pennsylvania, but it would have been impossible to
devise a tax that would operate on every part of the community
with exact equality.

The excise tax was not a lucrative source of revenue.
In the first three years the receipts were so small that it was
necessary to look elsewhere for possibilities of revenue. A
tax was placed on carriages, on the manufacture of snuff, sugar
refining and auction sales. By 1799, however, the excise tax on
distilled liquors had approached Hamilton's calculations and was
well developed by the time it was repealed in 1801. One thing we
owe to Hamilton: through his efforts the government made clear its
power to tax.

[31] _Ibid_, 492

Receipts of Excise:

1792	----	$209,000	1797	---- $575,000
1793	----	338,000	1798	---- 644,000
1794	----	274,000	1799	---- 779,000
1795	----	338,000	1800	----1,543,000
1796	----	475,000	1801	----1,582,000 [32]

In 1800, when Jefferson became President, his first
recommendation to Congress was to abandon at once all the internal revenue of the country. This was in fulfillment of the
party platform pledge. Immediately Hamilton wrote a series of
papers, under the name of Lucius Crassus, in an attempt to
prevent the action. The annual revenue from the excise tax
was by now approximately one million dollars.[33] Some of this
revenue was pledged for paying the interest and redeeming the
principal of the public debt. Furthermore, the Act of March 3,
1795, which matured and perfected the establishment of the
sinking fund, provided that any excess of revenue would become
a part of the sinking fund. The Act expressly declared that
"the moneys which are to constitute the fund shall inviolably
remain so appropriated and vested, until the redemption of the
debt shall be completely effected." Hamilton maintained that at
this period the country was passing from a state in which
neutrality had procured to our commerce and to the revenues
depending on it, a great and artificial increase, with every

[32] Dewey, P. 57
[33] Lodge, VIII, 252

reason to look for a decrease in the future. It would be rash
to abandon the valuable income from the excise, which by now was
firmly established. Since the revenues had been repeatedly
pledged to the payment of the public debt, "until the whole debt
shall be discharged with the single reservation that the government shall be at liberty to substitute other funds of equal
amount", Hamilton considered this a breach of contract.[34] This
would definitely give an appearance of instability in the plans
of a government. Since it involved the financial policy of
that government, there is no doubt that it would affect the
impressions of foreigners. Hamilton considered this an attempt
to establish a precedent ruinous to public credit, calculated to
prolong the burden of the debt, and to enfeeble the government.[35]

The excise, in spite of Hamilton's defense, was removed.
Gallatin, although for fully a decade previous to taking office
had worked for the abolition of the excise, was now reluctant
to recommend its repeal.[36] He realized that the import revenues
were not sufficient to meet the current expenses of the government and payment on the debt. In 1802, without Gallatin's approval, a bill was introduced by John Randolph for the repeal of
the excise. The loss of revenue was felt severely during the first
decade of the 19th century, especially in 1807 and 1809 after the

[34] Ibid, p. 269
[35] Ibid, p. 292
[36] Chien Tsanz Mai, Financial Policies of A. Gallatin

passage of the Embargo and Non-Importation Acts, when our import revenue fell off to such an extent that it was necessary to consider again the former source of revenue. Consequently, in 1812 Gallatin proposed the excise. It was not adopted, however, until many years later.

CHAPTER IV

HAMILTON'S CONTRIBUTION TO POLITICAL ECONOMY

It is a task of some magnitude to discuss Hamilton's
contribution to Political Economy and his place in the development of the American economic thought. In order to make a just
estimate, it is necessary to recall some fundamental facts.
When Hamilton wrote, Political Economy was in its infancy. It
was only with the then recent work of the Physiocrats and Adam
Smith that it had become a separate science with a more or less
systematized body of thought. Here in the United States due importance was not given it until the end of the first quarter of
the nineteenth century. Hamilton's only contact with the theoreti-
cal side of the subject was from tracts, pamphlets and books
brought over by friends, and from discussions with those states-
men of the country who had traveled to France and had been in-
doctrinated with the teachings of the Physiocrats. Of course,
much that he could not acquire from books was obtained by
observation of conditions in the America of his day.

We must further make the distinction between pure
science and applied science. Hamilton worked in a practical field.
His reports were monographs concerned primarily with administra-

tion and it is only by interpretation that they are interesting
as treatises on economic theory. The economic problems which confronted the nation, the public debt, money, a bank, the question
of manufactures, demanded urgent attention. As has been indicated,
Hamilton, with little originality but much judgment and wisdom,
introduced financial principles successful in England and applied
them to the solution of the country's financial problems. If we
consider contribution in the narrow sense of adding something new
to a subject, discovering principles, framing laws in production
and distribution, then Hamilton did none of these. He clarified
certain elements, confirmed or denied laws through research, and
combined induction and deduction, thereby contributing to method.
Yet, he did infinitely more than this. He solved the intricate
financial problems that faced the new nation and paved the way for
a sound national economic policy. It is true that he owed a debt
of gratitude to the many economic theorists who preceded him, but
it is a debt in a negative way only, inasmuch as these predecessors
pointed out what policies not to adopt in establishing his own
economic doctrines. By excluding the others, he made his own.

Finally, we must bear in mind that Hamilton was also a
political scientist, concerned with the development of the United
States into a great nation. To him, a strong central government

was a firm foundation on which to build economic principles. The
Federalist essays, which were written with the special purpose of
enunciating a political theory, show that such theory was nearly
as important to Hamilton as economic development. He realized
that no economic policies, such as he had in mind, could be
successful without a strong central government. A few of these
fundamental propositions as set forth in the Federalist papers
should be cited as Hamilton's index to a successful administration
of the political, social and economic welfare of the nation.

> A government ought to contain in itself every
> power requisite to the full accomplishment of
> the objects committed to its care, and to the
> complete execution of the trusts for which it
> is responsible, free from every other control
> but a regard to the public good and to the
> sense of the people.

Hamilton was confident that the government would "grow and flourish
in proportion to the quality and extent of the means concentrated
toward its formation and support."[1]

In order to be an effective agent the government would
have to be an animated, all-important factor in the lives of its
citizens, for

> a government continually at a distance and out
> of sight can hardly be expected to interest the
> sensations of the people .... The in-
> ference is that the authority of the Union, and
> the affections of the citizens towards it, will
> be strengthened rather than weakened by its

[1] H.C. Lodge, Works of Alexander Hamilton, II, 241

extension to what are called matters of internal concern and will have less occasion to
recur to force, in proportion to the familiarity
and comprehensiveness of its agency. 2

The same idea was again stressed.

The more the operations of the national authority are intermingled in the ordinary exercise
of the government, the more the citizens are
accustomed to meet with it in the common occurrences of their political life, the more it
is familiarized to their sight and to their
feelings, the further it enters into those
objects which touch the most sensitive chords,
and put in motion the most active springs of
the human heart, the greater will be the
probability that it will conciliate the respect
and attachment of the community. 3

The Constitution would have to be interpreted liberally

if it was to be used for the welfare of the nation for

it is impossible to foresee or define the
extent and variety of the national exigencies
or the correspondent extent and variety of
the means which may be necessary to satisfy
them. The circumstances that endanger the
safety of nations are infinite and for this
reason no constitutional shackles can wisely
be imposed on the power to which the care of
it is committed. 4

Although this philosophy of government formed the basis

of his economic activities, Hamilton was not entirely insensible

to economic theory. He read the leading theories, examined them

carefully, then adopted or discarded them as they met the particular

needs of the country or not. He paid no attention to the con-

ventional formulae, but thought his way to what seemed specifically

applicable to the United States. The errors, inconsistences and

2 Ibid, p. 214
3 Ibid, p. 213
4 Ibid, p. 181

exaggerations of predecessors were not spared criticism.

Hamilton's was the first written challenge to the laissez-faire system. The publication of Adam Smith's <u>Wealth of Nations</u> marked an epoch in economic thought. Self-interest, competition, private property, a natural order, a beneficent Providence -- were the basis of the Classical System. There was no doubt that the materialistic, utilitarian philosophy rampant in Europe had its repercussions in economics. Smith, imbued with this philosophy and observing conditions in England, published his reflections as economic laws. But Hamilton, when faced with the problems of economic policy, rejected Smith. Specialized in the realm of applied science, he detected fallacies inherent in Smith's teachings. Furthermore, Hamilton was conditioned by circumstances surrounding him. The United States was a new nation, with few manufactures, but a slightly developed agriculture, and no market. Were she to adopt Smith's axioms of economic policy, there would be no progress. England had developed her agriculture, her manufactures and commerce to the extent of her resources. In the latter part of the nineteenth century, according to Smith's observations, she was in a static state. This was not the condition of the United States. Extensive, unused, natural resources, an increasing population, a progressive spirit indicated a dynamic

state. Hamilton thus recognized the validity of Smith's maxims
for England, but a new set of economic principles would have to
be used in the United States, whose future economic development
seemed so promising.

In particular, Hamilton attacked "government passivity
and free trade." Government protection and regulation of trade
and industry was not only advocated but considered helpful and
essential. Emphasis was placed on the nation as an economic unit.
Government would be a good, not an evil. This does not mean that
Hamilton rejected all of Smith's theory. It is now obvious that
he read the Wealth of Nations carefully, admired the author, and
accepted and respected his criticism of the Physiocrats and
recognized the beneficial effects of the division of labor.

Hamilton likewise challenged the contentions of the
Physiocrats and their adherents. There was strong objection to
the development of manufactures from Jefferson and his colleagues.
Affected by the Physiocratic teachings, they contended that the
wealth of a nation depended on its attention to agriculture. To
this Hamilton answered, "The wealth of nations depends upon an infinite variety of causes. Situation, soil, climate, the nature of
the products, the nature of the government, the genius of its citizens,
the degree of intelligence they possess, the state of commerce,

of art, of industry,"[5] all determine it.

In proof of the fact that manufactures were just as
important as agriculture, Hamilton showed how they would furnish
a home market for agricultural products. Furthermore, manufactures
were absolutely necessary to a balanced economy, the goal of all
nations. Specifically, objection was made to the idea that manufactures gave no return equivalent to rent. But rent, in Hamilton's
opinion, was only another form of profit on capital. There was no
essential difference in the net return of agriculture and manufactures. The only possible difference would be that in manufactures,
profit goes to both owner and to the manager of the property; in
agriculture, profit goes to a single person who is usually both
owner and manager. The latter, we admit, is an erroneous notion of
rent.

Although Hamilton accepted none of the Physiocratic
doctrine, he thought highly of Turgot, and especially spoke favorably
of his financial policies.

We cannot say that Hamilton was a Mercantilist, for he did
not subscribe to all the teachings of this school either. The
doctrine that the wealth of nations ultimately was measured by the
amount of gold and silver in her treasury was attacked with the
following: "The intrinsic wealth of a nation is to be measured not

[5] Lodge, II, p. 163

by the abundance of precious metals contained in it, but by the
quantity of the products of its labor and industry."[6]

However, Hamilton's commercial and industrial policies
were Mercantilistic. A system of premiums, bounties and a protective tariff were the commercial policies of Colbert. They had
been successful in building French and English commerce and
industry; consequently, it was necessary to use those measures
in the United States.

Hamilton deserves great credit for his economic fore-
sight. The new laissez-faire philosophy was popular. As is the
case with a new theory, it might have been adopted by a new
country. But Hamilton sensed the impossibility of building a
nation without government assistance and direction. Although he
wrote no dissertation on the economic policies to be adopted in
a country in its different stages of production and progress,
he was undoubtedly the inspiration of such theory's incorporation
in List's National System.

Optimism was a characteristic feature of Hamilton's
economic philosophy. There was absolute certainty about the
government's ability to pay its obligations, past as well as
future. Hamilton contended that "Every system of Public Credit
must assume it as a fundamental principle that the resources of

[6] Ibid, III, 404

a country are equal to its probable exigencies and that it will possess ability to pay the debts which it contracts."[7]

A political philosophy, noted previously, was equally as important to the economic and social development of the United States.

These facts are stressed because they are fundamental to Hamilton's work as an economist. It is this philosophy of government, a zealous optimism, and an eclectic attitude towards economic schools, which Hamilton contributed to the subject of Political Economy. He was literally a Political Economist, believing both politics and economics to be interdependent. A strong central government aided by the cooperation and confidence of its citizens and by the use of tried and successful economic policies would insure a great nation.

Thus we conclude that although Hamilton had little personal interest in purely academic aspects of political economy, nevertheless, he furnished a valid criticism and correction of them and so helped to shape subsequent economic theory. The peculiar environmental conditions of the United States invited a reaction to the set principles of Smithian economics. Hamilton by his spirit and interpretation of economic doctrines paved the way for a broader and truer economics. He was the predecessor

[7] Ibid, II, 235

of the American School of Political Economy of which Daniel
Raymond, Matthew Carey, Henry C. Carey, Rae and List were
members. From the point of view of method and relation to
Classical Political Economy we might say that the liberal thought
of Hamilton served as a stimulus to the Historical School of
Roscher, Knies and Hildebrand.

BIBLIOGRAPHY

LOCATION OF REFERENCES CONTAINED IN THE HAMILTON MANUSCRIPTS

Library of Congress

Arbuthnot, John, Tables of Ancient Coins and Weights and Measures, 1727

Book of Rates (Of Customs and Valuations), Scotland Laws, Statutes, Etc. 1567-1625

Newton, Sir Isaac, Tables of Assays, Weights and Values of most Foreign Silver and Gold Coins, London, 1740

Lex Mercatoria Rediviva, or the Merchant's Directory -- London, Printed for the author by J. Moore and sold by E. Comyns, 1752

Kruse, Jurgen Elert, Allgemeiner und besonders hamburgischer contorist, Hamburg, 1771-1772

Johns Hopkins Library

Anderson, Adam, Annals of Commerce - A Historical and Chronological Deduction of the Origin of Commerce, London, 1787-1789

Price, Richard, State of the Public Debt of Great Britain.

Hume, David, Political Discourses.

Smith, Adam, Wealth of Nations

Harvard Library

The British negotiator; or, Foreign exchanges made perfectly easy -- Slack, Thomas (S. Thomas, pseudo.), London, J. Richardson, 1759?

London Bibliography

Kearsley Tax Duties which contain the Inland and Excise Duties

Kearsley, C, Kearsley's 6 penny tax tables including all the taxes imposed in the year 1791 and a variety of other acts of general concern, 1791, Royal Statistical Society.

Giraudeau, P., La Banque Rendu Facile aux Principales Nations de l'Europe, 1769, Goldsmith Library.

Leslie, Improvement of the Proposition of Hatton and Whitehurst, 1747 Hatton, E, Comes Commercii, or the Trader's Companion, etc. 2 vol. in one. Goldsmith Library

Higg's Bibliography

Tableau du Pair des Monnaies et des Changes des Principales Villes de l'
        Europe, Paris, 1757.

Parairi, John, Modern Universal Tables of the Monies, Weights and
        Measures of the World, translated into English, Dublin, 1756.

Partial Indentification

Poids ou Marc d'Or et d'Argent. Cite des Monnoyes. -- Grimaudet, F:
        Des Monnoyes augment, et dimins, du pris dicelles, etc.,
        1585, Goldsmith Library.

Unidentified

Commerce of Amsterdam, 6th Edition, 1744

Representation from the Merchants of Amsterdam respecting Gold Coins, 1750

PRIMARY SOURCES

Official Documents, Statutes

American Letters and Documents, 1652-1845 U.S. Miscellany

American State Papers. Finance

Benton, T.H., Abridgement of Debates of Congress, 10 vols. 1789-1850

Biographical Directory of American Congress, 1774-1927

Documents Relative to Manufactures in the United States, 22nd Congress, 1st.
        session, Ex. Doc. no. 308, II

Finance Reports, Reports of Secretary of Treasury from 1789-1849,in 6 vols.

Hamilton Manuscripts, Library of Congress, 109 vols.

Journals of Continental Congress 1774-1789, Washington 1904. Extracts
        from Journal and Ms. Reports of Continental Congress
        appear in International Monetary Conference 1878. Senate
        Ex. Doc. no. 58, 45th Congress, 3rd session, 1879. Also
        contains Coinage Reports of Morris and Jefferson, Reports of
        Board of Treasury and Ordinance on Coinage of Continental Congress.

Papers of Thomas Jefferson

Private Letter Book of Robert Morris

Tariff Acts Passed by Congress of the United States from 1789-1909

Tariff on Imports of United States, etc. and Free List together with
        Comparative Tables of Present and Past Tariffs. Report
        no. 12. Senate, 48th Congress, 1st session, Washington, 1884.

U.S. Census

U.S. Statutes at Large, 8 vols.

Wharton's Diplomatic Correspondence

CONTEMPORARY NEWSPAPERS AND MAGAZINES

Baltimore: Maryland Gazette
               Maryland Journal

Boston: Columbian Centinel
               Independent Chronicle

Charleston: City Gazette

Hartford: Courant

New Haven: Connecticut Gazette

New York: New York Daily Advertiser
               Commercial Advertiser
               Gazette of the United States
               New York Journal

Philadelphia: National Gazette
               Philadelphia Daily Advertiser
               General Advertiser
               Aurora
               American Museum
               Pennsylvania Pocket

Portsmouth: New Hampshire Gazette

Vermont: Spooner's Vermont Journal

SECONDARY SOURCES

Biographical

Atherton, Gertrude, The Conqueror, 36th printing 1936

Bailey, Ralph E., American Collossus, Lothrop, Lee, Shepperd & Co., 1933

Boutele, Lewis H., Alexander Hamilton, the Constructive Statesman

Bowers, Claude, Jefferson and Hamilton, Houghton, Mifflin Co., 1926

Culbertson, W.S., Alexander Hamilton, an Essay, 1911

Ellis, Edward S., Alexander Hamilton, 1903, New York

Ford, Henry J., Alexander Hamilton, Scribner's, 1920

Ford, P.L., The Federalist, 1890

Ford, P.L., Bibliotheca Hamiltonia, Knickerbocker Press, 1886.

Fox, Fontaine, A Study in Alexander Hamilton, Neale Pub., 1911

Hamilton, Allan McLane, Intimate Life of Alexander Hamilton, Scribner's, 1910

Hamilton, J.A., Reminiscences.

Hamilton, John C., Life of Alexander Hamilton, 1834-1840

Hamilton, John C., History of the Republic as Seen in the Writings of
     Alexander Hamilton, New York, 1857-1860.

Hicks, Howard, Alexander Hamilton, New York, 1928

Lodge, Henry Cabot, Alexander Hamilton, Houghton, Mifflin, Co. 1882.
     American Statesman Series.

Lodge, Henry Cabot, Works of Alexander Hamilton, 9 vols., 1885; 12 vols., 1904

Morse, John T. Jr., Life of Alexander Hamilton, 2 vols., Boston, Little,
     Brown & Co., 1876

Mulford, Roland, Political Theories of Alexander Hamilton, 1903

Oliver, Frederick S., Alexander Hamilton, an Essay in American Union, 1921

Renwick, James, Lives of John Jay and Alexander Hamilton, 1841

Riethmuller, C.J., Hamilton and His Contemporaries

Schouler, James, Alexander Hamilton, Small & Maynard Co., 1901

Shea, G., Alexander Hamilton, a Historical Study, 1877

Shea, G., Life and Epoch of Alexander Hamilton, Boston, Holton, Osgood & Co., 1879

Smertenko, Alexander Hamilton, Greenburg Press, 1932

Smucker, Samuel, Life and Times of Alexander Hamilton

Smyth, Clifford, Alexander Hamilton, the Little Lion of the Treasury, Funk and Wagnall's Co., 1866

Sumner, William G., Alexander Hamilton, N.Y. Dodd and Mead Co., 1890

Vandenburg, A.H., The Greatest American, Alexander Hamilton, 1921

Vandenburg, A.H., If Hamilton Were Here Today, 1927

Warshow, R.I., Alexander Hamilton, the First American Business Man, 1931

SECONDARY SOURCES

Financial: - General

Adams, Henry C., Public Debts, 2 vols, N.Y., 1887

Adams, Henry C., Taxation in the United States, 1789-1816, J.H.U. Studies,
    n.2,5,6

Bayley, Rafael A., History of National Loans of the United States from
    July 4, 1776 - June 30, 1880, (pp.295-486) n. 7 10th census
    of U.S., 1880.

Bogart, E.L. and Kawles, Wm. A., Trial Bibliography and Outline of
    Lectures in the Financial History of the United States

Bolles, A.S., American Finance with Chapters on Money and Banking, N.Y., 1901
    Financial History of the United States (2nd Ed., N.Y. 1884-1886) 3 vols

Breck, Historical Sketch of Continental Paper Money

Bronson, Henry, Historical Account of the Connecticut Currency Continental
    Money and Finances of Revolution, New Haven Colony Historical
    Society Papers, Vol. 1, 1865

Bullock, Charles J., Essay on Monetary History of the United States, 1775-1789.
    Madison Bulletin Ess., etc. Vol. 1, no.2

DeKnight, Wm. F., History of Currency of Country and of the Loans of U.S.
    from the Earliest Period to June 30th, 1900. 2nd Ed. Washington, 1900.

Dewey, Davis R., Financial History of the United States, 1931, Longmans, Green Co

Douglas, Charles, Financial History of Massachusetts, Col. V., Studies in Hist.
    Ess. and Pub. law, IV, 1

Dunbar, Charles F., Laws of the United States Relating to the Currency,
    Finance and Banking from 1789-1891, Boston, 1891

Felt, J.B., Historical Account of Massachusetts Currency, Boston, 1839

Gallatin, Albert, Sketch of American Finance, 1796-1798

Gauge, William G., Short History of Paper Money and Banking in the
    United States, Philadelphia, 1833

Grayson, Theodore, Leaders and Periods of American Finance, John Wiley & Son.

Hickox, John H., History of Bills of Credit of New York, Albany, 1866

Holt, Bryon W., Continental Currency. Sound Money, Vol. 5, no. 7   1898

Kearny, John Watts, Sketch of American Finances, 1789-1835, New York, 1887.

Phillips, Henry Jr., Historical Sketches of Paper Currency in America,
        2 vols. 1865-1866

Paine, Thomas, Writings of Thomas Paine

Potter and Rider, Bills of Credit in Rhode Island

Schuckers, J.W., Brief Account of the Paper Money of the Revolution,
        Philadelphia, 1874

Schultz and Cain, Financial Development of the United States

Sumner, William G., History of American Currency, 1870, Rev. 1884

Upton, Jacob, Money in Politics, Boston, 1884

Walker, Francis A., Money, New York, 1891

Financial: - Specific

Sinking Fund

Anderson, Annals of Commerce

Barton, J.H., Sinking Funds, Reserve Funds and Depreciation, London, 1922

Brisco, N.A., Economic Policy of Robert Walpole

Chandler, A.D.,"Amortization", Am. Rev. v.3, 1913

Elliot, Jonathan, Funding System of the United States and Great Britain, Washington, 1845

Gould, Nathan, Essay on Public Debt of the Kingdoms, Doc. no. 15, H.R. 28th Congress, 1st. session, 1726

Love, R.A., Federal Financing, A Study of the Methods Employed by the Treasury in its Borrowing Operations, Col. V. Studies H. Ess. and Pub. Law. no 337 N.Y. 1931

McCulloch, R., Taxation

Price, Richard, Appeal to the Public on the Subject of the National Debt, 1774 Observations on Reversionary Payments.

Ross, E.A., Sinking Funds, Am. Es. Ass. Public Money, v. 7, no. 4,5, 1892, Baltimore

Withers, William, Retirement of National Debt, Col. V. Studies Hist., Ess. and Pub. Law, no. 374 N.Y., 1932.

Tontine

Moulin, Jacques, Des Tontines, 1903, Paris

Annuities

Kopf, Edwin W.,"Early History of Annuities", Casual Actuarial Society Proceedings, 225-226, XIII, 1926-1927

Money and Banking

Andreades, A., Histoire de la Banque d'Angleterre, 2 vols., Paris, 1904 by C. Meredith, 1909.

Bradford, F.A., Money and Banking, 1935

Carey, Matthew, Essays on Banking

Clark, Matthew and Hall, David, Legislative and Documentary History of
the Bank of the United States, 1832

Conant, Charles A., History of Modern Banks of Issue, N.Y., 1897, 4th Ed., 1911
Chap. 13-15, Bank of U.S.

Dowrie, G.W., American Monetary and Banking Policies, 1930

Dunbar, Charles F., Chapters on the Theory and History of Banking, 1896

Francis, Joseph, History of the Bank of England, 1818, Euclid Publishing
Company, London

History of Banking in the Leading Nations, 4 vols. N.Y., 1896, Journal
of Commerce Publications.

Hoggson, N.F., Epochs in American Banking

Holdsworth, Th., First and Second Banks of the United States, Nat. Mon.
Comm. Publ.

Konkle, Alva, Thomas Willing; the First American Financial System

Knox, John J., History of Banking in the United States

Lewis, Lawrence, History of the Bank of North America, Philadelphia, 1882

Muhleman, M.L., History of Monetary and Banking Systems, N.Y., 1908

Nevins, Allan, Bank of New York and Trust Company, 1934

Sumner, William G., History of Banking in the United States

White, Horace, Money and Banking Illustrated by American History, 1902

Willis, Parker and Berkhardt, B.H., Foreign Banking Systems, N.Y., 1929

Coinage

Breckenridge, S.P., Legal Tender, a study of English and American
Monetary History

Carothers, Neil, Fractional Money, 1930, John Wiley & Son

Hepburn, A. Bartow, History of Coinage and Currency in the United States,
N.Y., 1903

Laughlin, J. Lawrence, History of Bimettalism in the United States, 4th Ed., 189

Linderman, Henry R., Money and Legal Tender in the United States, 1877

Seybert, Adam, Statistical Annals. Philadelphia, 1818. 1789-1818

Watson, David, History of American Coinage, N.Y., 1899

Industry and Commerce

Andrews, Charles McLean,"Colonial Commerce", American Historical Review,
        Vol. 20, no. 1, pp. 43-63, Oct., 1914.

Bagaill, Wm. R., Textile Industries in the United States (1639-1810),
        Cambridge, 1893

Blodget, L,"Economica", Statistical Manual of U.S.A., Washington, 1800
        Am. stat. man.

Bolles, A.S., Industrial History of the United States, Conn. 1879

Clark, Victor S., History of Manufactures in the United States, 1607-1860,
        Washington, 1916

Cole, Arthur H., Industrial and Commercial Correspondence of Alexander
        Hamilton, Chicago, 1928

Coman, Katherine, Industrial History of the United States, N.Y.,1911

Cowdrick, E.S., Industrial History of the United States

Davies, J.L., Essays on the Earlier History of American Corporations,
        Mass., 1917

Elliott, Orrin Leslie, Tariff Controversy in the United States, 1789-1833,
        with summary of period before adoption of Constitution. Leland
        Stanford, Jr., U. Monogs. Hist. and Ess., Sept., 1892

Ely, Richard, Studies in the Evolution of Industrial Society, 1913

Goss, John D., History of Tariff Administration in the United States,
        Studies in Hist. Ess. and Public Law of Columbia College, 1891

Hill, William, First Stages of the Tariff Policy in the United States,
        Am. Ec. Pub., Vol. 8, no. 6 (vol. 1 no. 2) Baltimore, 1893

Howe, Frank C., Taxation and Taxes in the United States. Under Internal
        Revenue System, 1896.

Pitkin, Timothy, Statistical View of the Commerce of the U.S.A., 1835

Rabbeno, Ugo, American Commercial Policy, 2nd Ed. rev. London, 1892.

Smith and Seligman, Commercial Policies of the United States, 1892, Leipzig

Sumner, William G., Lectures on the History of Protection in the United
        States, N.Y., 1884

Taussig, R.H., <u>Tariff History of the United States,</u> 7th Ed., 1923
        <u>Protection to Young Industries as Applied in the United States,</u>
        N.Y., 1884

Taylor, R.I., <u>Outline of American Industrial History,</u> 1915

Wright, C.D., <u>Industrial Evolution of the United States,</u> 1902

Young, Edward, Special Report on Customs, Tariff Legislation of
        the United States, Washington, 1874, Bureau of Statistics
        Treasury Dept.

Articles

Bourne, Edward,"Alexander Hamilton and Adam Smith,"<u>Quarterly Journal
        of Economics,</u> 1893, VIII, 328-344

Dunbar, Charles, "Economic Science in America, 1776-1875", <u>North
        American Review,</u> 1876

Lunt, D.C., "Hamilton as a Political Economist", <u>Journal of Political
        Economy,</u> III, 239-310; 1894-1895

Historical

Adams, James Truslow, Jeffersonian Principles, Boston, 1928

Adams, James Truslow, Hamiltonian Principles, Boston, 1928

Adams, Randolph G., Political Ideas of the American Revolution, Trinity
        College Press, 1922

Andrews, Charles, Colonial Self-Government, 1863
        Colonial Background of the American Revolution, 1863

Bancroft, George, History of the United States, 6 vols, 1882-1885,
        Appleton & Co.

Bassett, John, Federalist System, N.Y., 1906 (Am. Nation Series)

Beard, Charles A., Economic Origins of Jeffersonian Democracy, N.Y., 1915
        Economic Interpretation of the Consitution of the United States, 1913
        American Government and Politics, N.Y., 1931
        Economic Basis of Politics, N.Y., 1934
    Smith, H.E. - "Idea of National Interest", N.Y. 1934
    Beard, M.A. - Rise of American Civilization, 2 vols., 1927

Beck, James, The Constitution of the United States, England, 1922

Becker, Carl, Declaration of Independence, Harcourt, Brace & Co., 1922
        Eve of the Revolution, Chronicle of Am. Series

Callender, J.T., History of the United States for the Year 1796

Channing, Edward, History of the United States, 6 vols., N.Y. 1905-1925
        Hart, A., Guide to Study of American History, 1896

Cheyney, Edward, European Background of American History, N.Y. 1904

Coxe, Tench, View of U.S.A., 1794-1795

Farrand, Livingston, Basis of American History, N.Y., 1904

Fiske, John, Critical Period of American History (1783-1789), N.Y., 1888

Gibbs, George (ed.), Memories of Administrations of Washington and
        John Adams edited from papers of Oliver Wolcott (vol.2, N.Y., 1846)

Gordy, J.P., History of Political Parties in the United States, 3 vols,
        Ohio, 1895

Griswold, R.W., The Republican Court, N.Y., 1879

Hamilton, John C., History of the United States as Traced in the Writings of Alexander Hamilton, 7 vols, 4th Ed. 1879

Hart, Albert, American History Told by Contemporaries, 4 vols.

Hildreth, Richard, History of the U.S.A., 6 vols, N.Y. 1849-1852

Hockett, Homer, Political and Social History of the United States, Macmillan, 1931

Holst, Herman Edward von, Constitutional and Political History of the United States, 7 vols, 1877-1892.

Jameson, T., American Revolution Considered as a Social Movement

Lecky, W.E.H., History of England in 18th Century, 8 vols, 1878, Appleton and Co. American Revolution

McDonald, William, Select Documents Illustrative of the History of the United States

MacIlwain, Charles H., American Revolution, a Constitutional Interpretation

McLaughlin, Andrews, Confederation and the Constitution, N.Y., 1905, American Nation series, Vol. II

McMasters, J.B., History of the People of the United States from the Revolution to the Civil War, 1783-1861, 8 vols., 1885-1916

Nevins, Allen, American States during and after the Revolution (1775-1789), N.Y., 1924

Parrington, V.L., "The Colonial Mind", Vol. I, Main Currents of Am. Lit. (1871-1929

Schlesinger, A.M., Colonial Merchants and the American Revolution, N.Y., 1918

Schouler, James, History of the United States under the Constitution, 1783-1877, 7 vols.

Simpson, Joseph, Hamiltonianism vs. Jeffersonianism, 1904, T.H. Harworth & Sons.

Thompson, History of the United States

Trevelyan, G.A., American Revolution, 3 vols, 1909, Longmans, Green & Co.

Tucker, George, History of the United States

Tyler, Lyon, England in America

Van Tyne, Charles, American Revolution, Am. Nation Series, vol. 9, 1902 Causes of War of Independence, Houghton, Mifflin Co., 1922

Walker, Francis A., Making of a Nation, 1783-1817, N.Y., 1895

Wilson, Woodrow, History of the American People, 5 vols, 1902

Winsor, Justin, Narrative and Critical History of America, 8 vols, 1884-1889

Miscellaneous

Adams, Henry, Works of Albert Gallatin, 3 vols., 1879

Ames, Seth, Works of Fisher Ames, 2 vols, Boston, 1854

Bowers, Claude, Jefferson and Hamilton

Brissot de Warville, J.P., New Travels in the United States, 1788

Chinard, Gilbert, Jefferson, 1929, Boston

Davis, John, Travels of Four and One-half Years in U.S.A. , 1799-1802, N.Y.,1909

Eliot, Debates in the Constitutional Convention

Ford, Worthington C., Works of Thomas Jefferson, 12 vols. (1904-1905)

Giles, William B. Works, Miscellany

Grayson, Theodore, Leaders and Periods of American Finance, N.Y., 1932

Greene, H.T., Works of H.T. Greene

Hirst, Margaret G., Life of Frederick List and Selections from His
        Writings, London, 1909

Hume, David, Political Discourses
        Essays and Treatises on Several Subjects, new ed. 1828

Hunt, Gaillard, Writings of James Madison, 9 vols, N.Y. 1900-1910

Hutcheson, Harold, Tench Coxe

Jay, Life of Jay

Kaplan, A.D.H., Henry Charles Carey, Johns Hopkins Studies in History
        and Political Science, 49. Baltimore, 1931

Liancourt, Dua de la Rochefoucauld, Travels through U.S.A., London, 1799

List, Frederick, National System of Political Economy, translated by
        G.A. Matile, Philadelphia, 1856

Maclay, William, Journal of 1789-1791, N.Y., 1927, Ed. by E.S. Maclay

Monaghan, Frank, Life of Jay, 2 vols.

Oberholtzer, E.P., Robert Morris, Patriot and Financier, N.Y. 1903

Roosevelt, Theodore, Gouveneur Morris (American Statesman Series), Boston, 1899

Rowe, Kenneth, Matthew Carey, Johns Hopkins University Studies in
    History and Political Science, Baltimore, 1933

Smith, Adam, Inquiry into the Nature and Causes of the Wealth of Nations, 1776

Sparks, Life of Washington

Stevens, John Austin, Albert Gallatin, Boston, 1899

Sumner, Wm. G., Financier and Finances of the American Revolution

Twining, Thomas, Travels in America 100 Years Ago, N.Y., 1893

Wansey, Henry, Journal of Excursion to U.S.A. in the Summer of 1794,
    London, 1796

Webster, Peletiah, Political Essays on the Nature and Operation of Money, 1797

DR. MILDRED OTENASEK
206 Harper House
Baltimore, Maryland
21210

Ph.D. - Johns Hopkins University

A.B. - College of Notre Dame of Maryland

Professor of Economics and Political Science
College of Notre Dame of Maryland
1964 - _____

Associate Professor of Economics
Trinity College, Washington , D.C.
1940 - 1954

Democratic National Committeewoman, Maryland, 1956 - 1980.

President: United Democratic Women's Clubs of Maryland, 1955 - 1957

Vice-Chairman: Democratic State Central Committee of Maryland
1948 - 1957.

Member of Policy Committee of Democratic National Committee, 1971.

Member of Credentials Committee for 1964 and 1968 Conventions.

Member of Allocation of Delegates Committee for 1968 Democratic
National Convention.

Member of Site Committee for 1964 Democratic National Convention.

Member of Arrangements Committee for 1960 Democratic National
Convention.

Delegate to 1956, 1960, 1964, 1968 and 1972 Democratic National
Convention.

Delegate to Democratic Conference on Organization and Policy,
Mini-Convention in Kansas City, 1974.

Member of Vice-Presidential Selection Commission, 1973.

Member of Fisher Commission, 1972 and 1975.

Member of James Commission, 1970.

Co-Chairman of Status of Women Commission, 1964-1966.

Past member of Governor's Reapportionment Committee.

Past member of Port Authority Committee.

Chairman of Equal Employment Opportunities Commission for Baltimore City, 1960-1962.

Dissertations in American Economic History

An Arno Press Collection

1977 Publications

Ankli, Robert Eugene. **Gross Farm Revenue in Pre-Civil War Illinois.** (Doctoral Dissertation, University of Illinois, 1969). 1977

Asher, Ephraim. **Relative Productivity, Factor-Intensity and Technology in the Manufacturing Sectors of the U.S. and the U.K. During the Nineteenth Century.** (Doctoral Dissertation, University of Rochester, 1969). 1977

Campbell, Carl. **Economic Growth, Capital Gains, and Income Distribution: 1897-1956.** (Doctoral Dissertation, University of California at Berkeley, 1964). 1977

Cederberg, Herbert R. **An Economic Analysis of English Settlement in North America, 1583-1635.** (Doctoral Dissertation, University of California at Berkeley, 1968). 1977

Dente, Leonard A. **Veblen's Theory of Social Change.** (Doctoral Dissertation, New York University, 1974). 1977

Dickey, George Edward. **Money, Prices and Growth;** The American Experience, 1869-1896. (Doctoral Dissertation, Northwestern University, 1968). 1977

Douty, Christopher Morris. **The Economics of Localized Disasters:** The 1906 San Francisco Catastrophe. (Doctoral Dissertation, Stanford University, 1969). 1977

Harper, Ann K. **The Location of the United States Steel Industry, 1879-1919.** (Doctoral Dissertation, Johns Hopkins University, 1976). 1977

Holt, Charles Frank. **The Role of State Government in the Nineteenth-Century American Economy, 1820-1902:** A Quantitative Study. (Doctoral Dissertation, Purdue University, 1970). 1977

Katz, Harold. **The Decline of Competition in the Automobile Industry, 1920-1940.** (Doctoral Dissertation, Columbia University, 1970). 1977

Lee, Susan Previant. **The Westward Movement of the Cotton Economy, 1840-1860:** Perceived Interests and Economic Realities. (Doctoral Dissertation, Columbia University, 1975). 1977

Legler, John Baxter. **Regional Distribution of Federal Receipts and Expenditures in the Nineteenth Century:** A Quantitative Study. (Doctoral Dissertation, Purdue University, 1967). 1977

Lightner, David L. **Labor on the Illinois Central Railroad, 1852-1900:** The Evolution of an Industrial Environment. (Doctoral Dissertation, Cornell University, 1969). 1977

MacMurray, Robert R. **Technological Change in the American Cotton Spinning Industry, 1790 to 1836.** (Doctoral Dissertation, University of Pennsylvania, 1970). 1977

Netschert, Bruce Carlton. **The Mineral Foreign Trade of the United States in the Twentieth Century:** A Study in Mineral Economics. (Doctoral Dissertation, Cornell University, 1949). 1977

Otenasek, Mildred. **Alexander Hamilton's Financial Policies.** (Doctoral Dissertation, Johns Hopkins University, 1939). 1977

Parks, Robert James. **European Origins of the Economic Ideas of Alexander Hamilton.** (M. A. Thesis, Michigan State University, 1963). 1977

Parsons, Burke Adrian. **British Trade Cycles and American Bank Credit:** Some Aspects of Economic Fluctuations in the United States, 1815-1840. (Doctoral Dissertation, University of Texas, 1958). 1977

Primack, Martin L. **Farm Formed Capital in American Agriculture, 1850-1910.** (Doctoral Dissertation, University of North Carolina, 1963). 1977

Pritchett, Bruce Michael. **A Study of Capital Mobilization, The Life Insurance Industry of the Nineteenth Century.** (Doctoral Dissertation, Purdue University, 1970). Revised Edition. 1977

Prosper, Peter A., Jr. **Concentration and the Rate of Change of Wages in the United States, 1950-1962.** (Doctoral Dissertation, Cornell University 1970). 1977

Schachter, Joseph. **Capital Value and Relative Wage Effects of Immigration into the United States, 1870-1930.** (Doctoral Dissertation, City University of New York, 1969). 1977

Schaefer, Donald Fred. **A Quantitative Description and Analysis of the Growth of the Pennsylvania Anthracite Coal Industry, 1820 to 1865.** (Doctoral Dissertation, University of North Carolina, 1967). 1977

Schmitz, Mark. **Economic Analysis of Antebellum Sugar Plantations in Louisiana.** (Doctoral Dissertation, University of North Carolina, 1974). 1977

Sharpless, John Burk, II. **City Growth in the United States, England and Wales, 1820-1861:** The Effects of Location, Size and Economic Structure on Inter-urban Variations in Demographic Growth. (Doctoral Dissertation, University of Michigan, 1975). 1977

Shields, Roger Elwood. **Economic Growth with Price Deflation, 1873-1896.** (Doctoral Dissertation, University of Virginia, 1969). 1977

Stettler, Henry Louis, III. **Growth and Fluctuations in the Ante-Bellum Textile Industry.** (Doctoral Dissertation, Purdue University, 1970). 1977

Sturm, James Lester. **Investing in the United States, 1798-1893:** Upper Wealth-Holders in a Market Economy. (Doctoral Dissertation, University of Wisconsin, 1969). 1977

Tenenbaum, Marcel. **(A Demographic Analysis of Interstate Labor Growth Rate Differentials;** United States, 1890-1900 to 1940-50. (Doctoral Dissertation, Columbia University, 1969). 1977

Thomas, Robert Paul. **An Analysis of the Pattern of Growth of the Automobile Industry:** 1895-1929. (Doctoral Dissertation, Northwestern University, 1965). 1977

Vickery, William Edward. **The Economics of the Negro Migration 1900-1960.** (Doctoral Dissertation, University of Chicago, 1969). 1977

Waters, Joseph Paul. **Technological Acceleration and the Great Depression.** (Doctoral Dissertation, Cornell University, 1971). 1977

Whartenby, Franklee Gilbert. **Land and Labor Productivity in United States Cotton Production, 1800-1840.** (Doctoral Dissertation, University of North Carolina, 1963). 1977

1975 Publications

Adams, Donald R., Jr. **Wage Rates in Philadelphia, 1790-1830.** (Doctoral Dissertation, University of Pennsylvania, 1967). 1975

Aldrich, Terry Mark. **Rates of Return on Investment in Technical Education in the Ante-Bellum American Economy.** (Doctoral Dissertation, The University of Texas at Austin, 1969). 1975

Anderson, Terry Lee. **The Economic Growth of Seventeenth Century New England:** A Measurement of Regional Income. (Doctoral Dissertation, University of Washington, 1972). 1975

Bean, Richard Nelson. **The British Trans-Atlantic Slave Trade, 1650-1775.** (Doctoral Dissertation, University of Washington, 1971). 1975

Brock, Leslie V. **The Currency of the American Colonies, 1700-1764:** A Study in Colonial Finance and Imperial Relations. (Doctoral Dissertation University of Michigan, 1941). 1975

Ellsworth, Lucius F. **Craft to National Industry in the Nineteenth Century:** A Case Study of the Transformation of the New York State Tanning Industry. (Doctoral Dissertation, University of Delaware, 1971). 1975

Fleisig, Heywood W. **Long Term Capital Flows and the Great Depression:** The Role of the United States, 1927-1933. (Doctoral Dissertation, Yale University, 1969). 1975

Foust, James D. **The Yeoman Farmer and Westward Expansion of U.S. Cotton Production.** (Doctoral Dissertation, University of North Carolina at Chapel Hill, 1968). 1975

Golden, James Reed. **Investment Behavior By United States Railroads, 1870-1914.** (Doctoral Thesis, Harvard University, 1971). 1975

Hill, Peter Jensen. **The Economic Impact of Immigration into the United States.** (Doctoral Dissertation, The University of Chicago, 1970). 1975

Klingaman, David C. **Colonial Virginia's Coastwise and Grain Trade.** (Doctoral Dissertation, University of Virginia, 1967). 1975

Lang, Edith Mae. **The Effects of Net Interregional Migration on Agricultural Income Growth:** The United States, 1850-1860. (Doctoral Thesis, The University of Rochester, 1971). 1975

Lindley, Lester G. **The Constitution Faces Technology:** The Relationship of the National Government to the Telegraph, 1866-1884. (Doctoral Thesis, Rice University, 1971). 1975

Lorant, John H[erman]. **The Role of Capital-Improving Innovations in American Manufacturing During the 1920's.** (Doctoral Thesis, Columbia University, 1966). 1975

Mishkin, David Joel. **The American Colonial Wine Industry:** An Economic Interpretation, Volumes I and II. (Doctoral Thesis, University of Illinois, 1966). 1975

Winkler, Donald R. **The Production of Human Capital:** A Study of Minority Achievement. (Doctoral Dissertation, University of California at Berkeley, 1972). 1977

Oates, Mary J. **The Role of the Cotton Textile Industry in the Economic Development of the American Southeast:** 1900-1940. (Doctoral Dissertation, Yale University, 1969). 1975

Passell, Peter. **Essays in the Economics of Nineteenth Century American Land Policy.** (Doctoral Dissertation, Yale University, 1970). 1975

Pope, Clayne L. **The Impact of the Ante-Bellum Tariff on Income Distribution.** (Doctoral Dissertation, The University of Chicago, 1972). 1975

Poulson, Barry Warren. **Value Added in Manufacturing, Mining, and Agriculture in the American Economy From 1809 To 1839.** (Doctoral Dissertation, The Ohio State University, 1965). 1975

Rockoff, Hugh. **The Free Banking Era: A Re-Examination.** (Doctoral Dissertation, The University of Chicago, 1972). 1975

Schumacher, Max George. **The Northern Farmer and His Markets During the Late Colonial Period.** (Doctoral Dissertation, University of California at Berkeley, 1948). 1975

Seagrave, Charles Edwin. **The Southern Negro Agricultural Worker:** 1850-1870. (Doctoral Dissertation, Stanford University, 1971). 1975

Solmon, Lewis C. **Capital Formation by Expenditures on Formal Education, 1880 and 1890.** (Doctoral Dissertation, The University of Chicago, 1968) 1975

Swan, Dale Evans. **The Structure and Profitability of the Antebellum Rice Industry:** 1859. (Doctoral Dissertation, University of North Carolina at Chapel Hill, 1972). 1975

Sylla, Richard Eugene. **The American Capital Market, 1846-1914:** A Study of the Effects of Public Policy on Economic Development. (Doctoral Thesis, Harvard University, 1968). 1975

Uselding, Paul John. **Studies in the Technological Development of the American Economy During the First Half of the Nineteenth Century.** (Doctoral Dissertation, Northwestern University, 1970). 1975

Walsh, William D[avid]. **The Diffusion of Technological Change in the Pennsylvania Pig Iron Industry, 1850-1870.** (Doctoral Dissertation, Yale University, 1967). 1975

Weiss, Thomas Joseph. **The Service Sector in the United States, 1839 Through 1899.** (Doctoral Thesis, University of North Carolina at Chapel Hill, 1967). 1975

Zevin, Robert Brooke. **The Growth of Manufacturing in Early Nineteenth Century New England.** 1975